HOW TO DRAW LIKE HOKUSAI

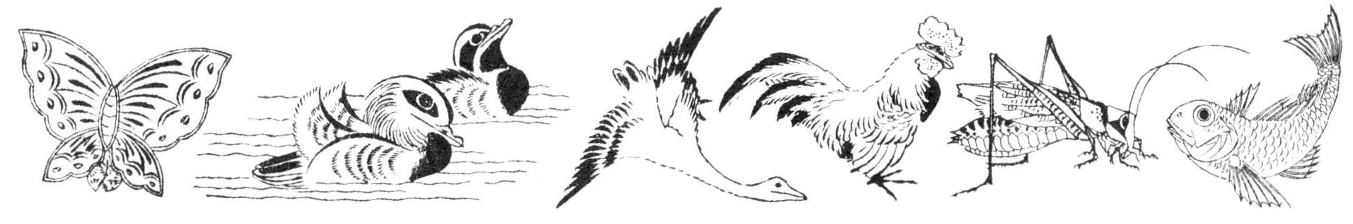

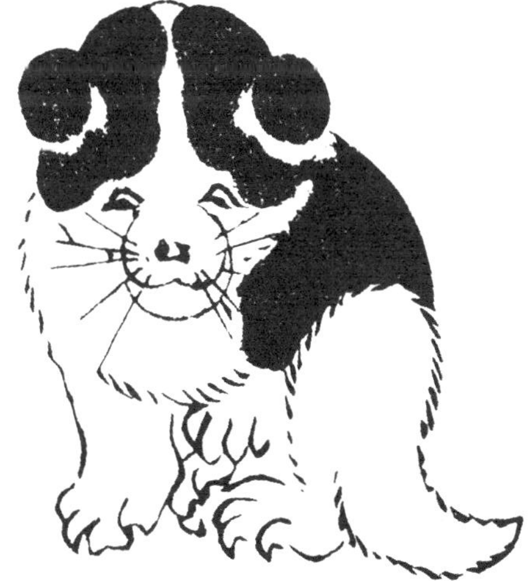

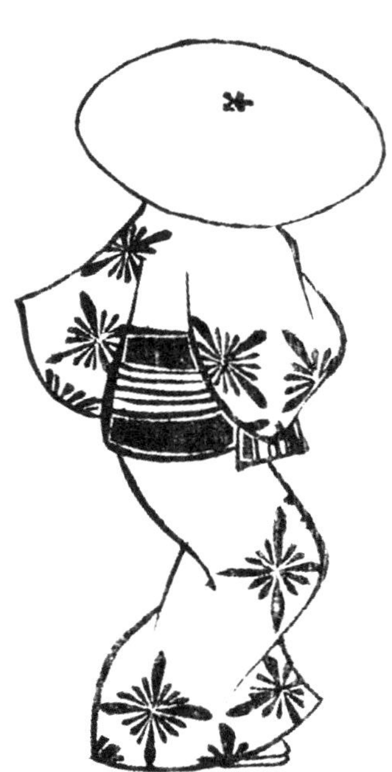

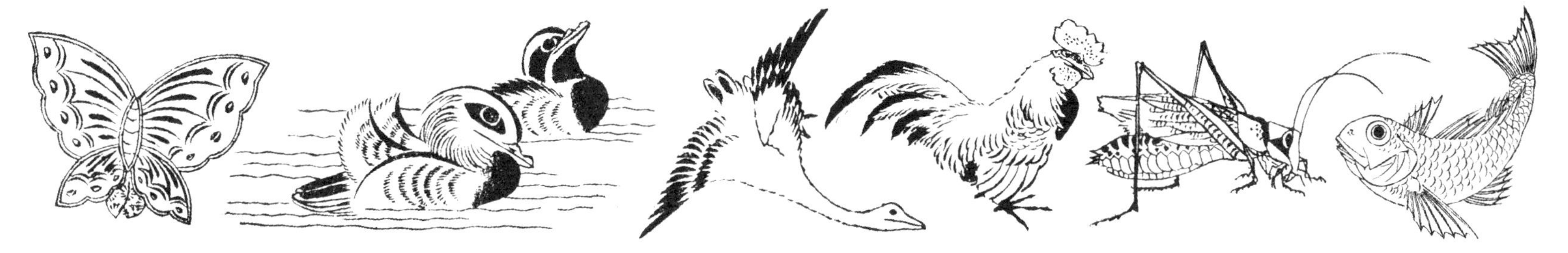

HOW TO DRAW LIKE HOKUSAI

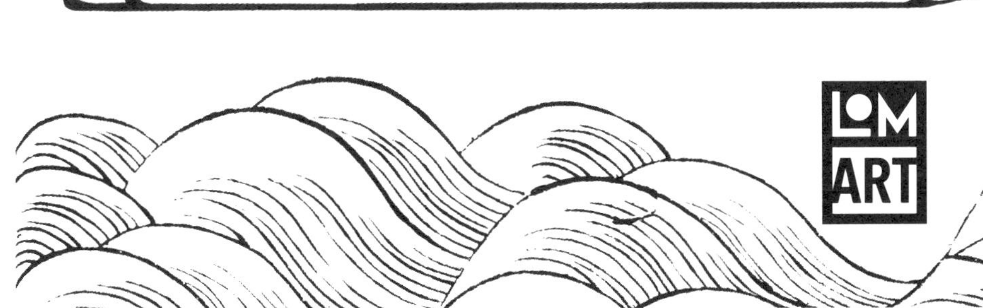

LOM ART

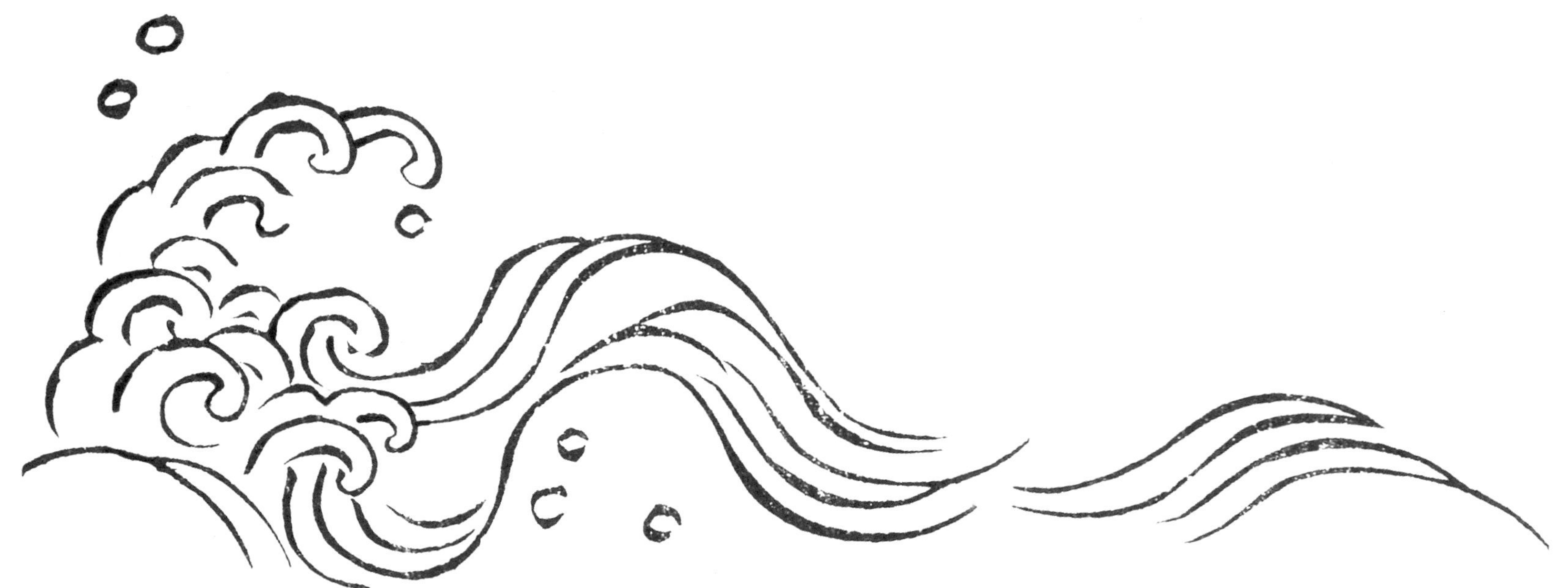

Introduction

Katsushika Hokusai, today known simply as 'Hokusai', is renowned for his instantly recognizable prints, including the iconic *The Great Wave Off Kanagawa*. During his prolific artistic career he produced many thousands of prints, paintings, sketches and illustrations.

Included in his work were a number of drawing tutorials, in which he shared a method for creating art in his very own style. These volumes presented step-by-step breakdowns on how to draw figures, animals, plants, landscapes and much more besides.

Within this book you'll find a lovingly presented selection of those lessons, with newly restored sketches and additionally created steps to make them easier to follow than ever before. So sit down with a pen and some paper, and enjoy emulating the work of arguably Japan's greatest grand master.

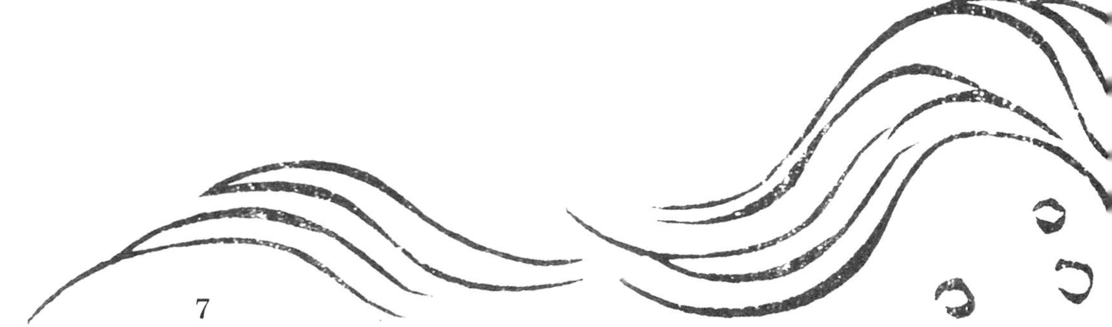

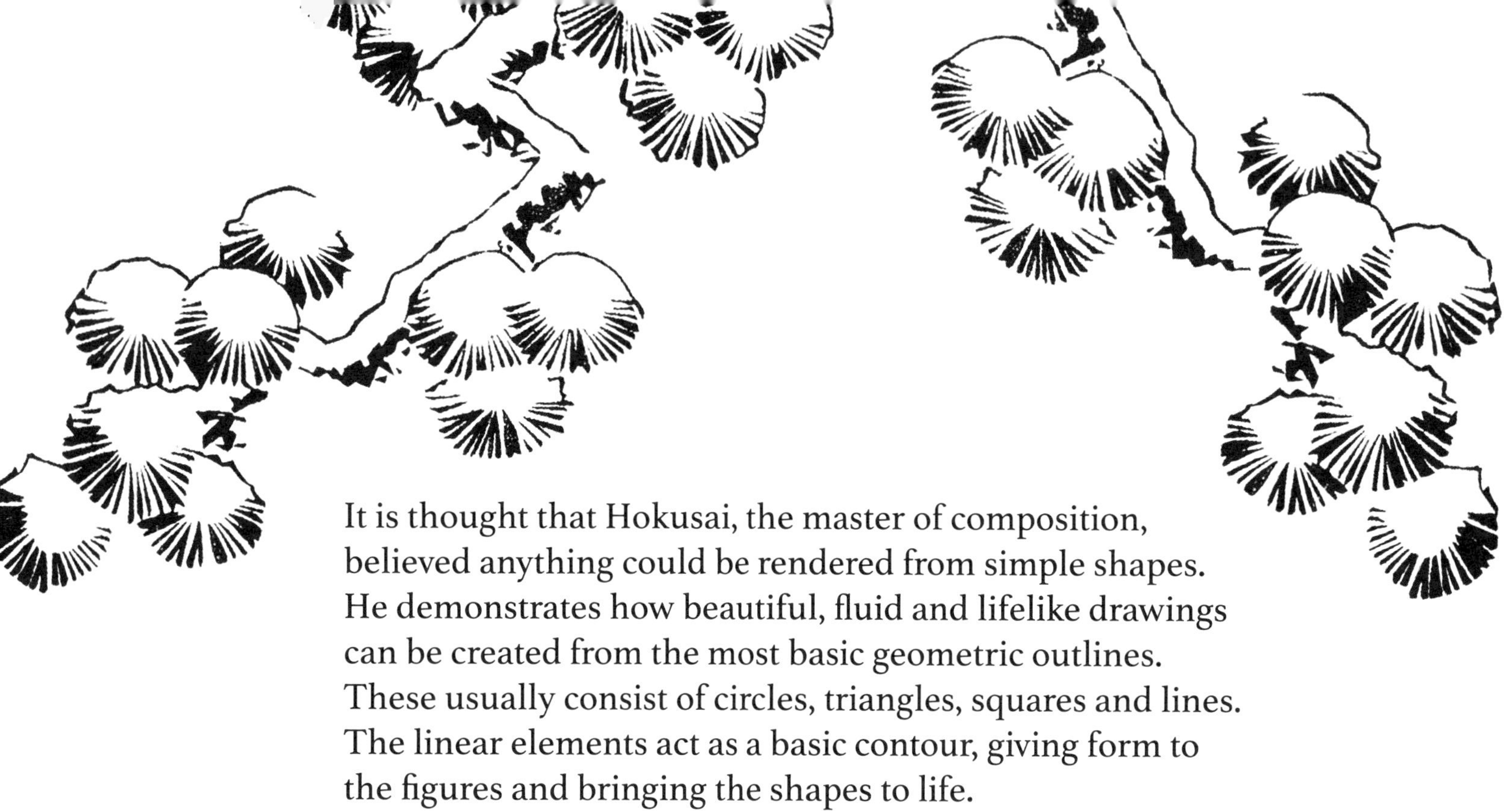

It is thought that Hokusai, the master of composition,
believed anything could be rendered from simple shapes.
He demonstrates how beautiful, fluid and lifelike drawings
can be created from the most basic geometric outlines.
These usually consist of circles, triangles, squares and lines.
The linear elements act as a basic contour, giving form to
the figures and bringing the shapes to life.

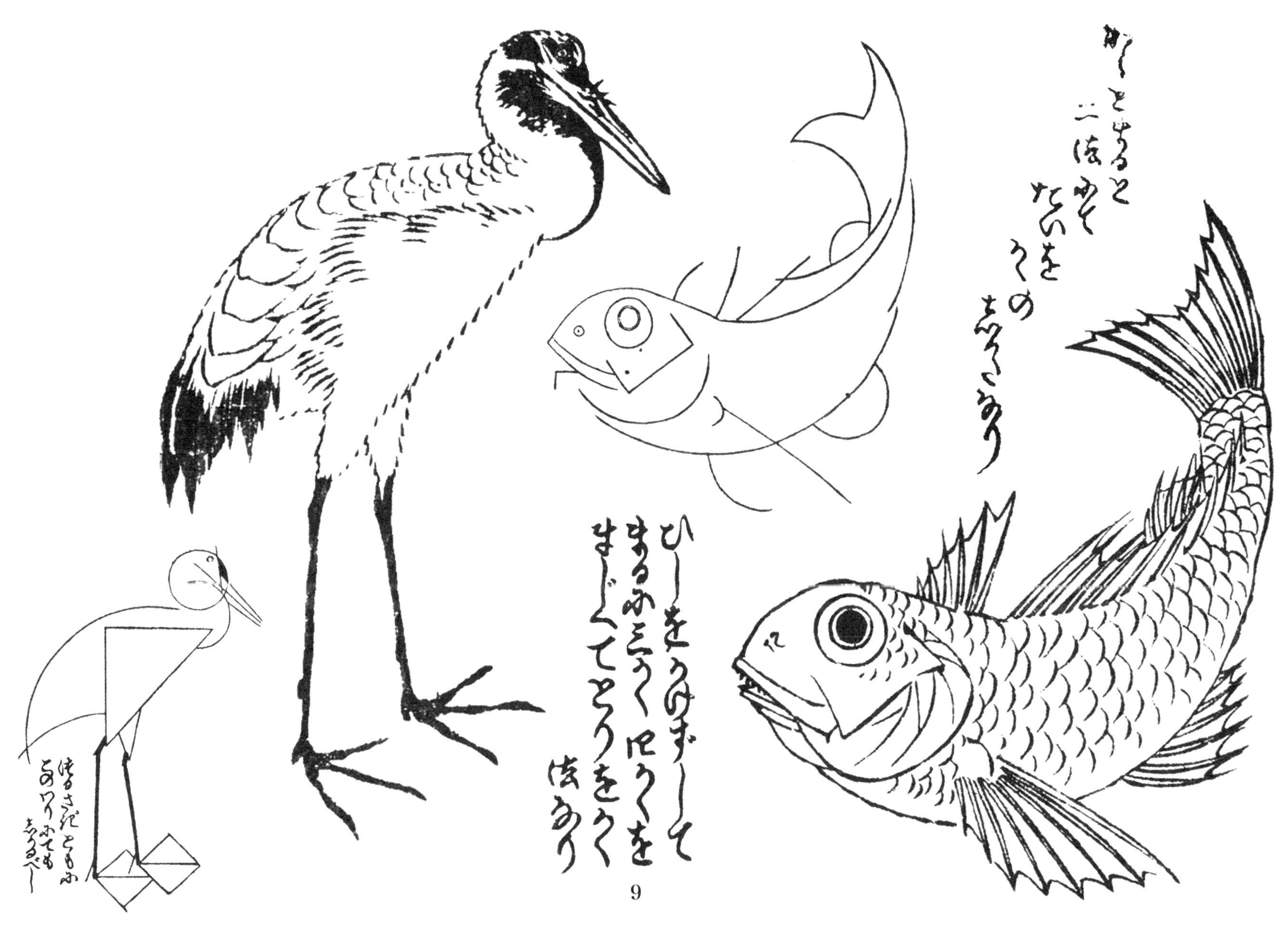

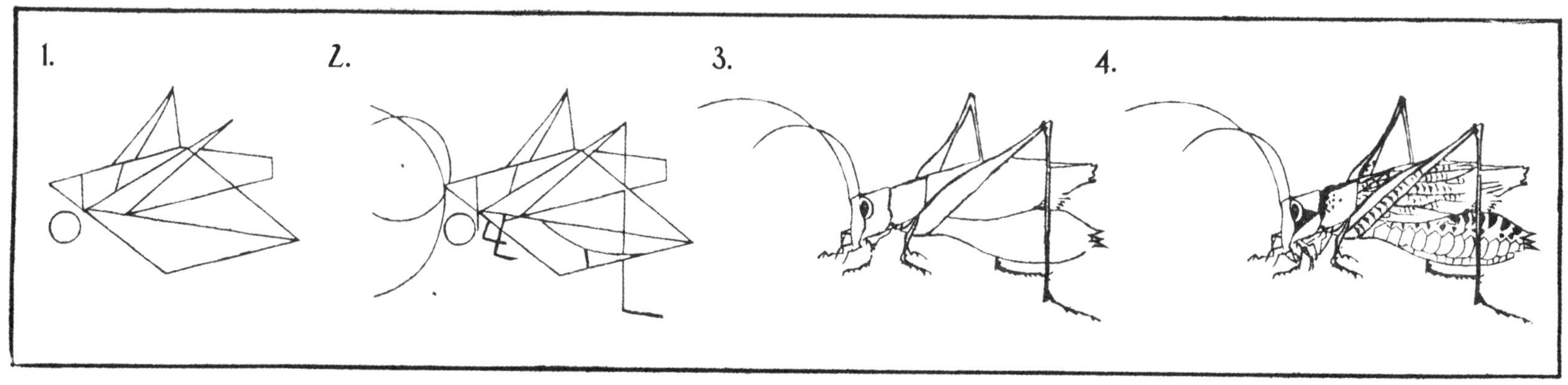

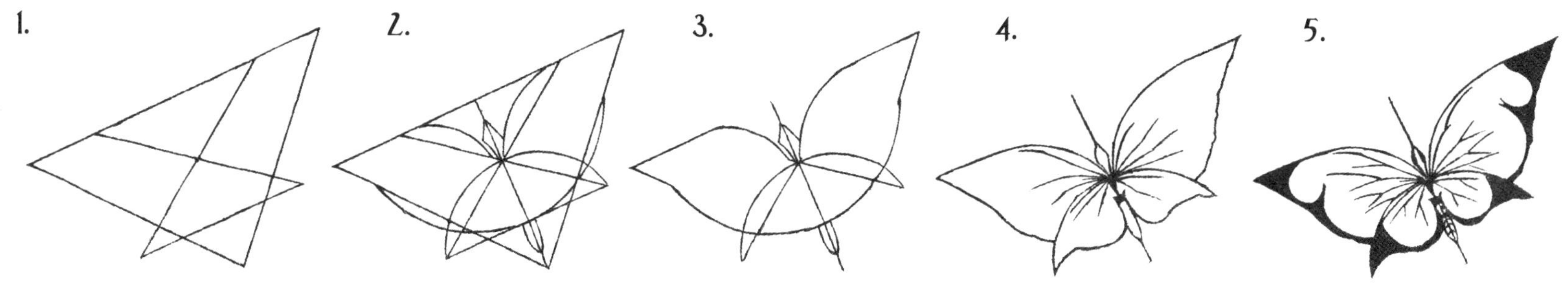

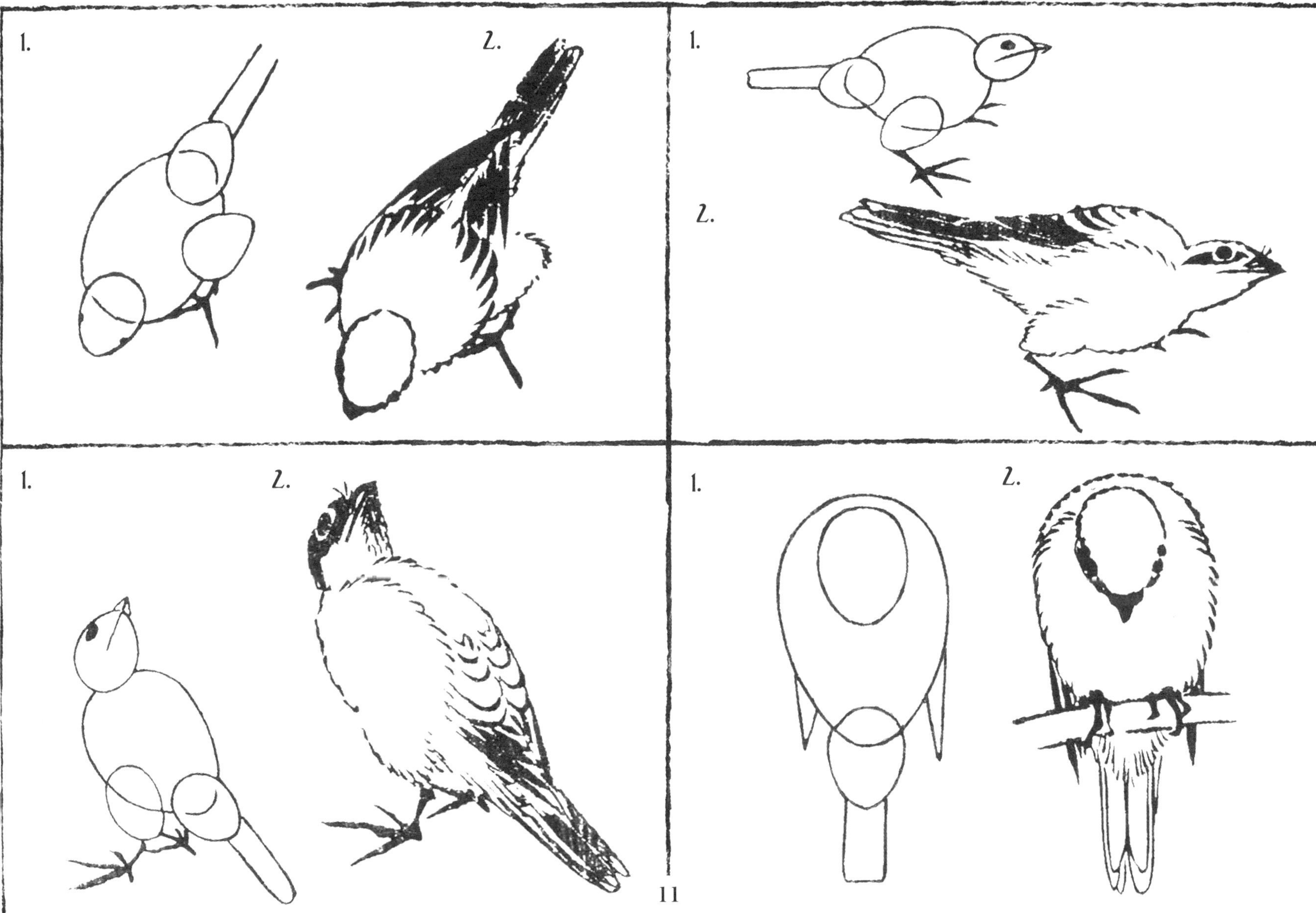
1.
2.
1.
2.
1.
2.
1.
2.

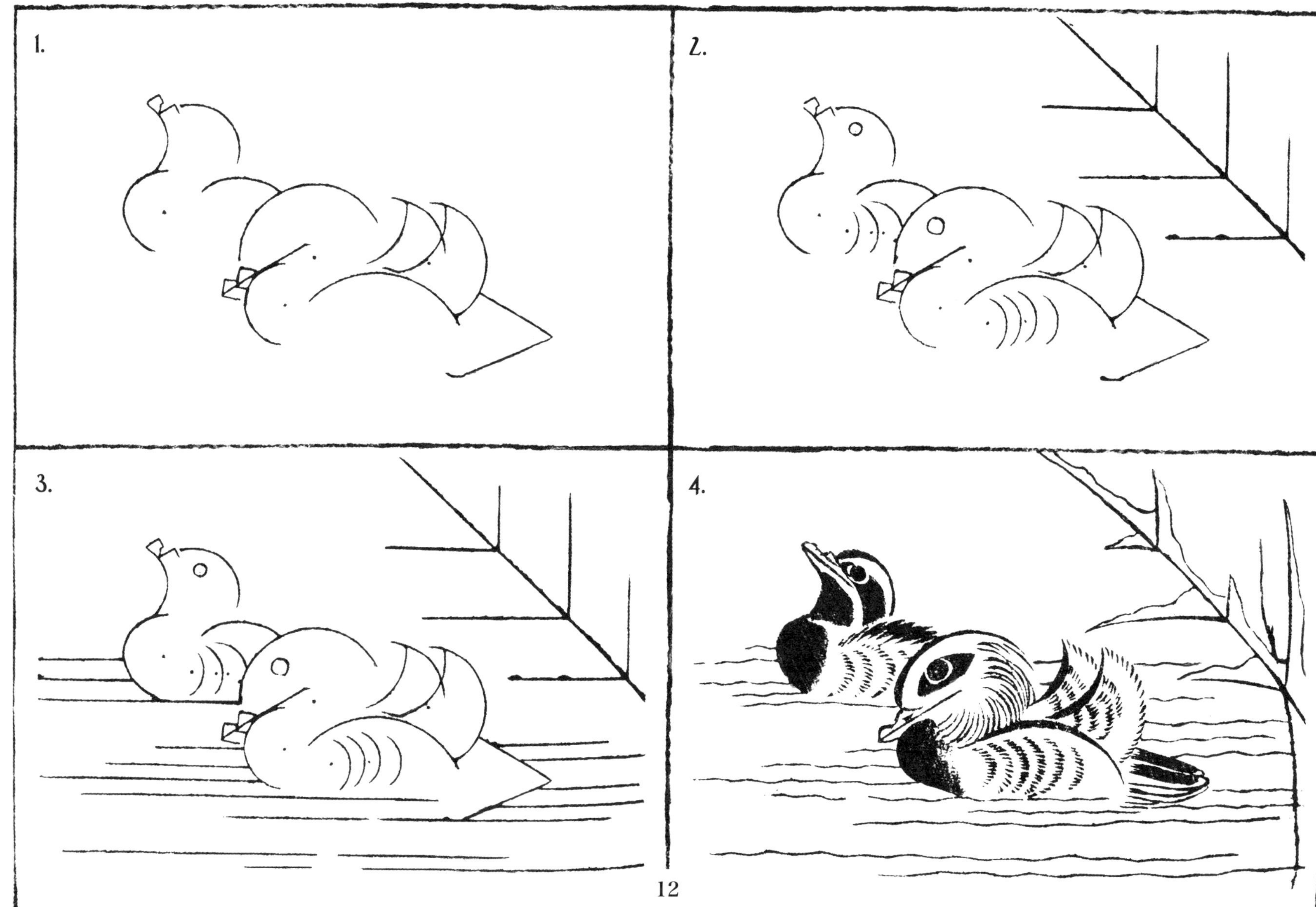
1.
2.
3.
4.
12

1.

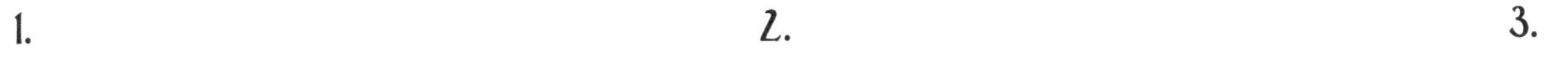

2.

3.

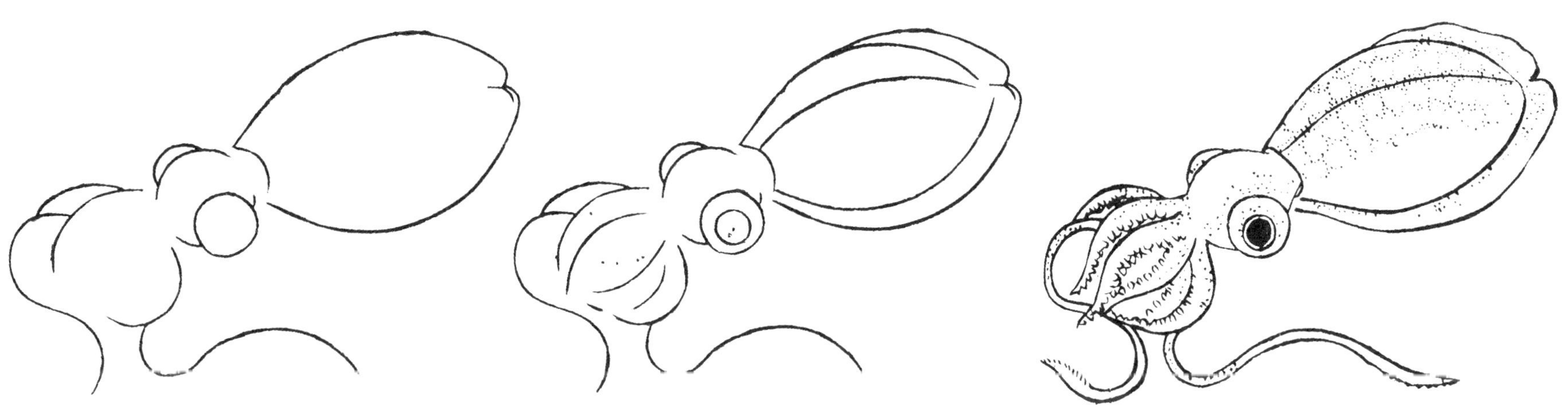

1. 2. 3. 4.

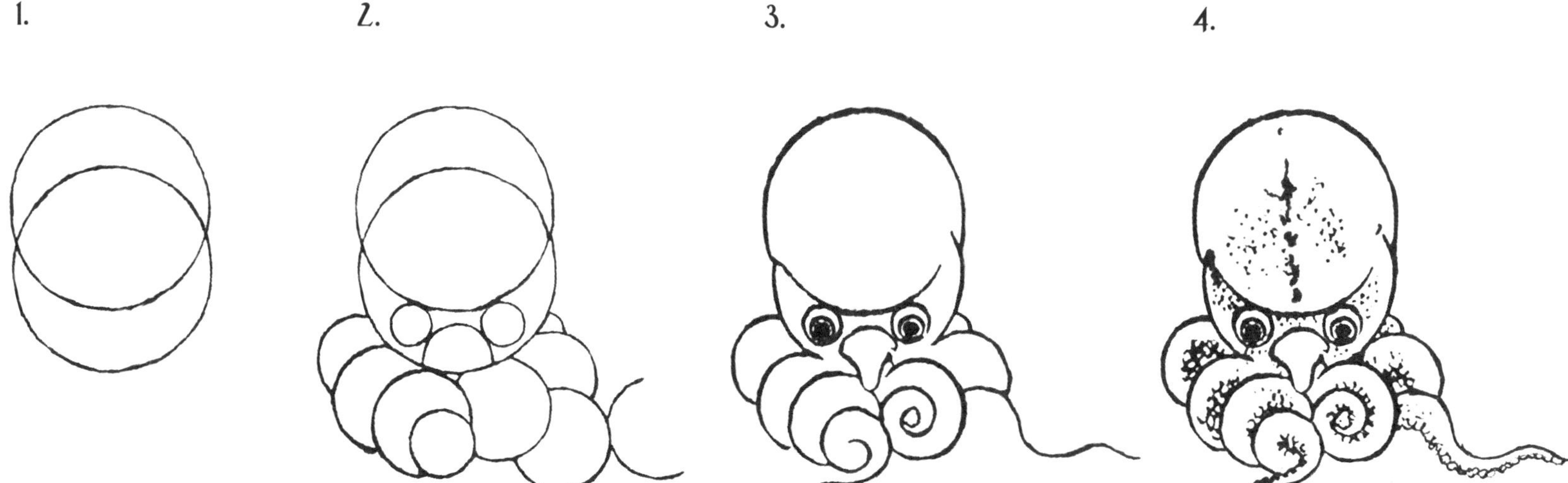

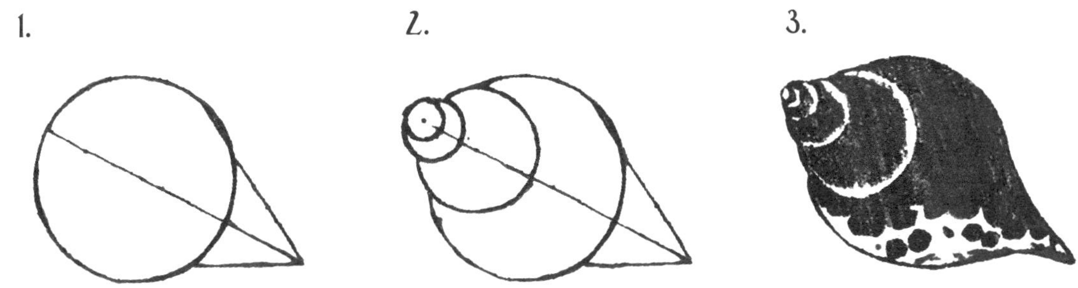

1.
2.
3.

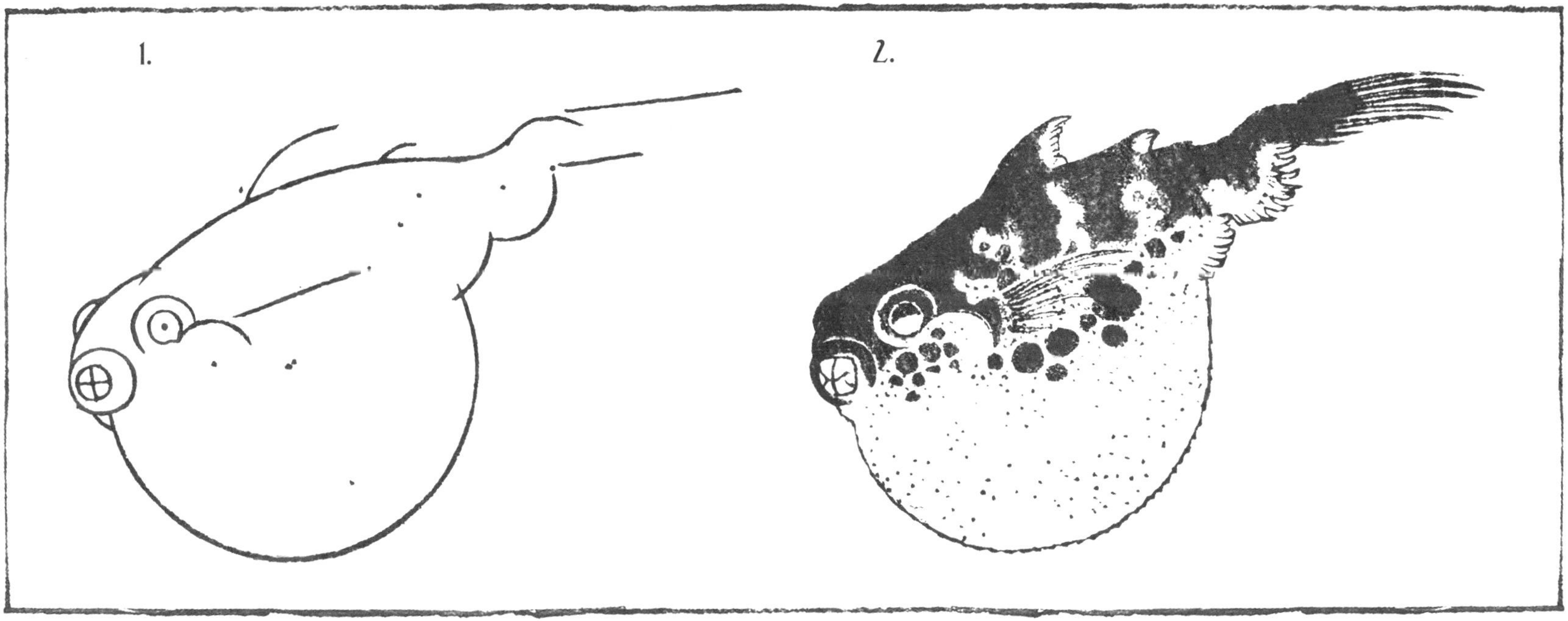

1.
2.

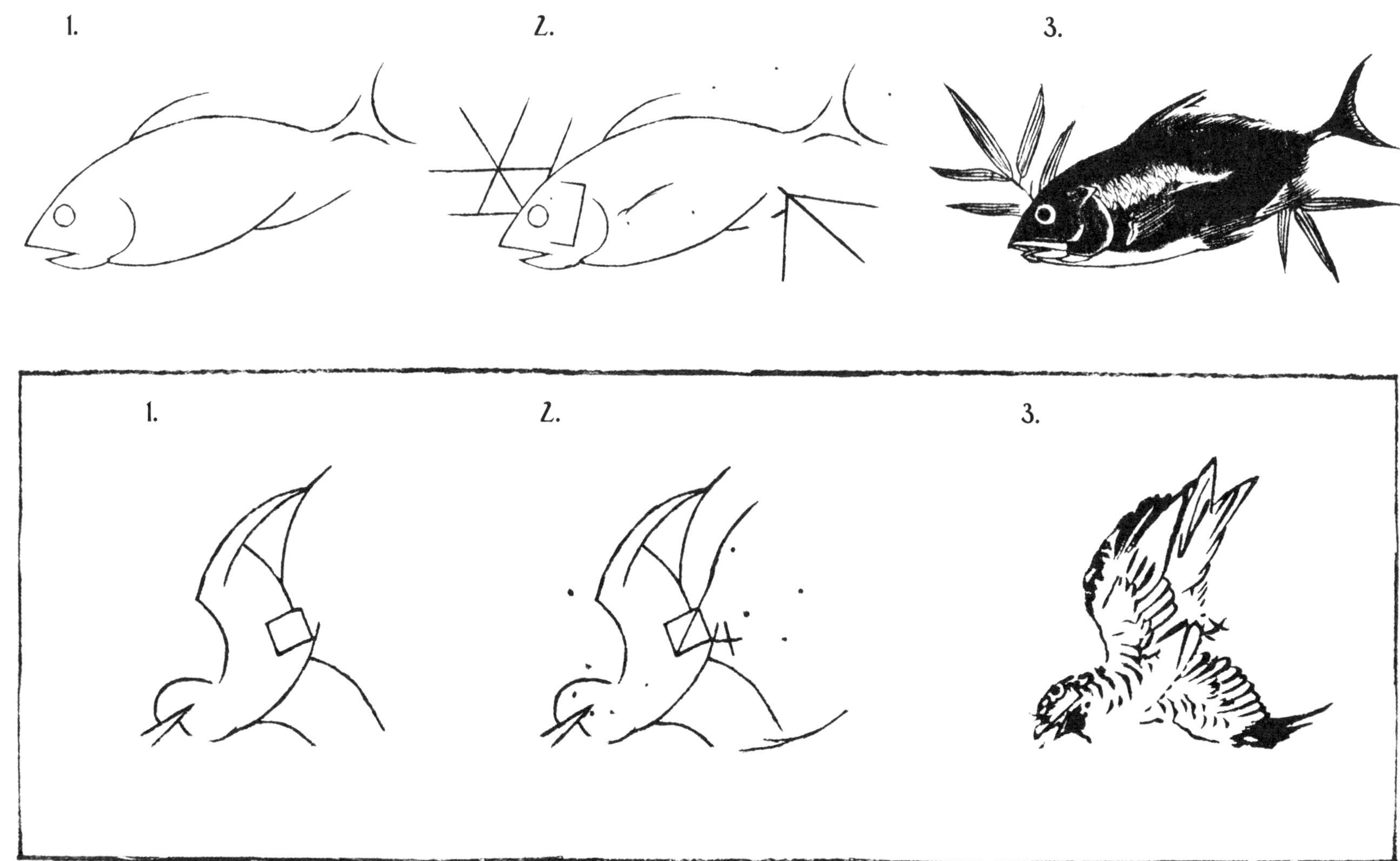

1.
2.
3.
1.
2.
3.

1.

2.

3.

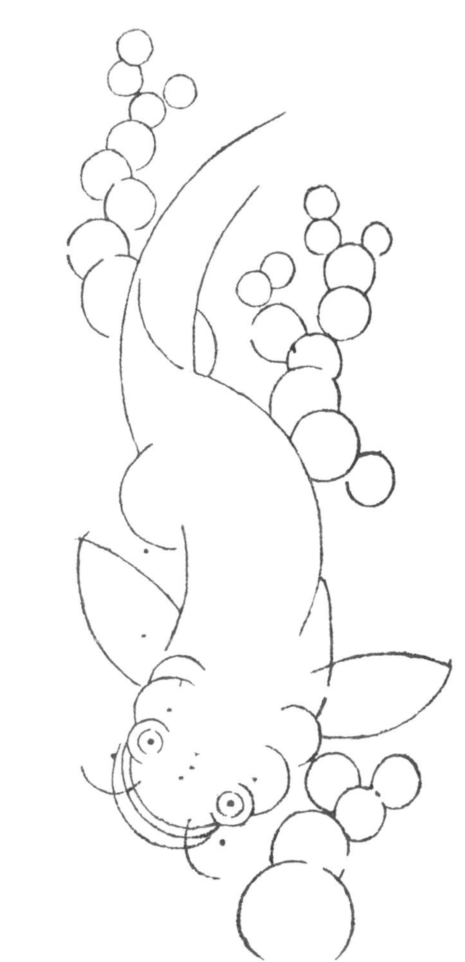
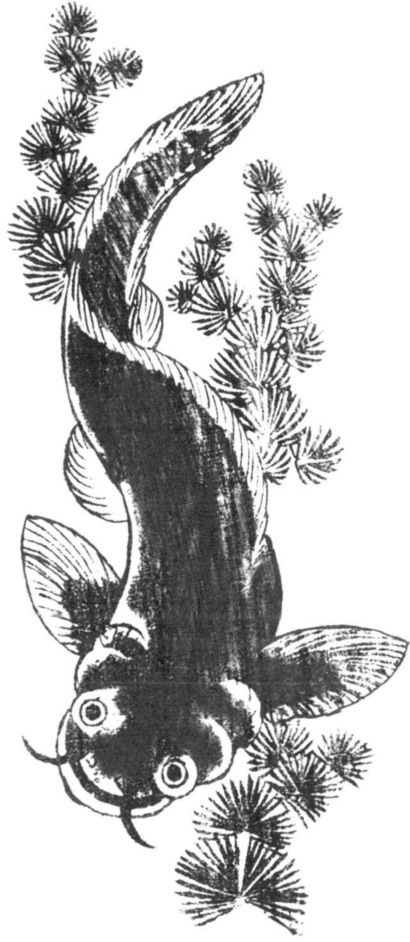

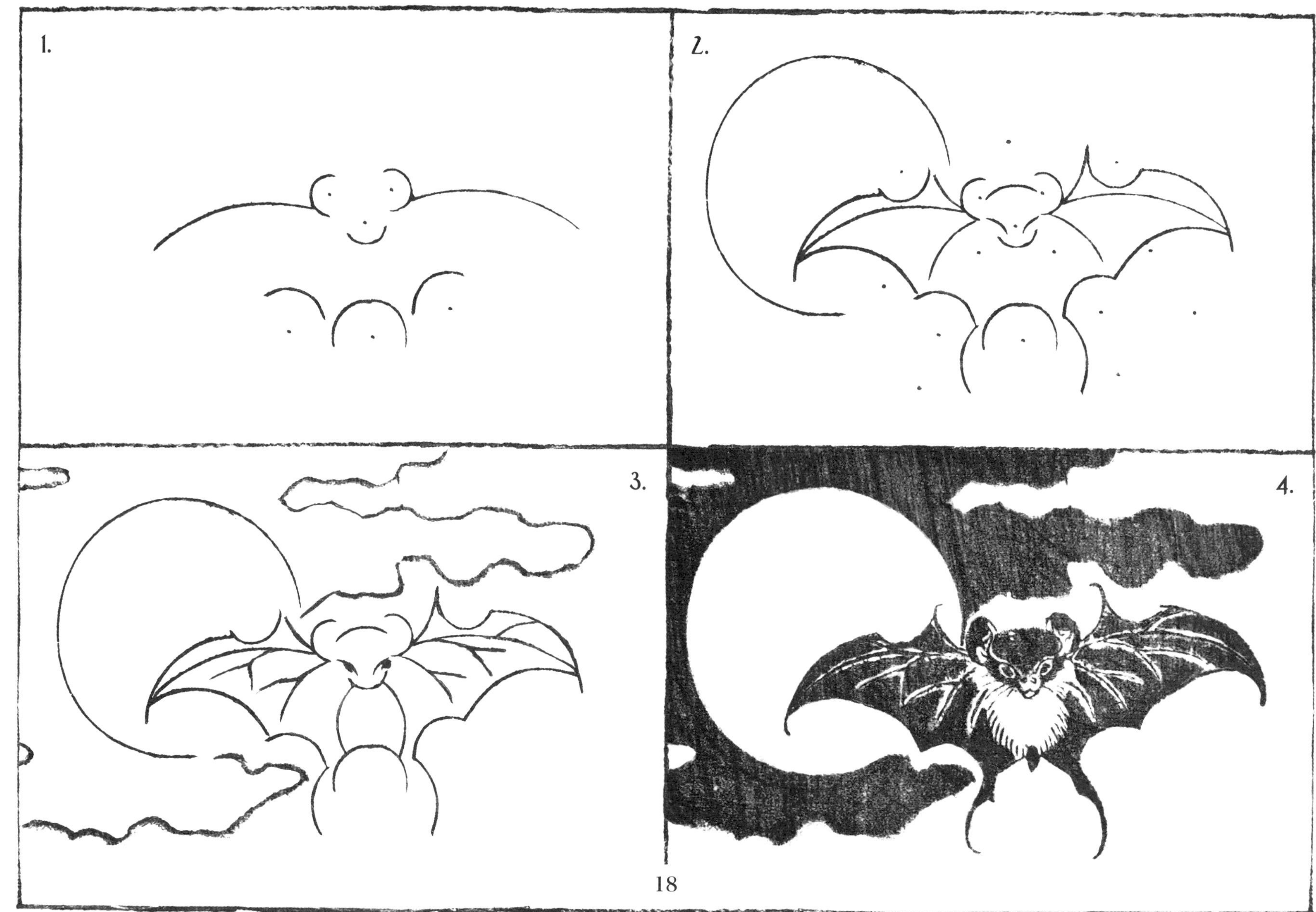

1.
2.
3.
4.

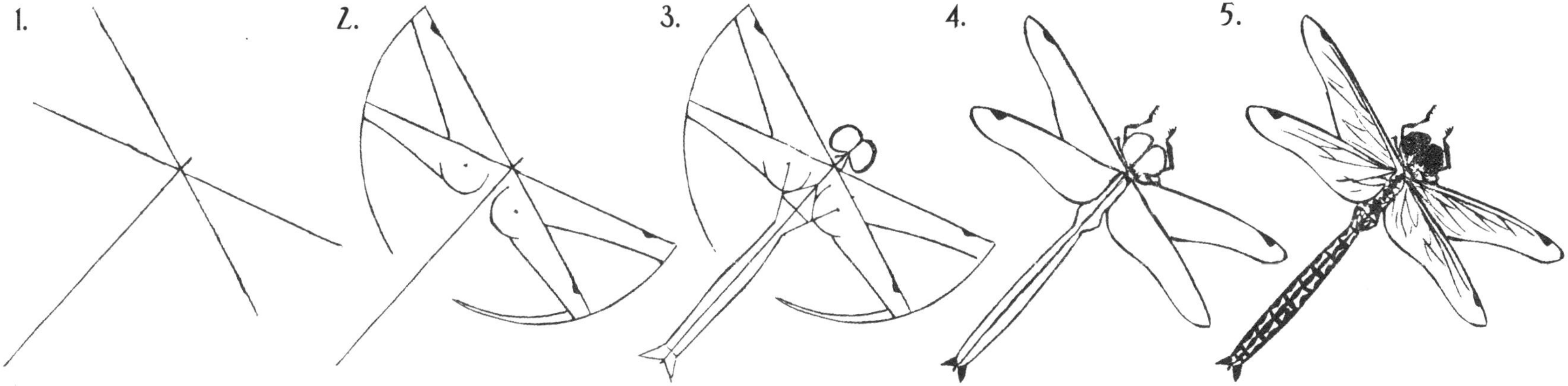

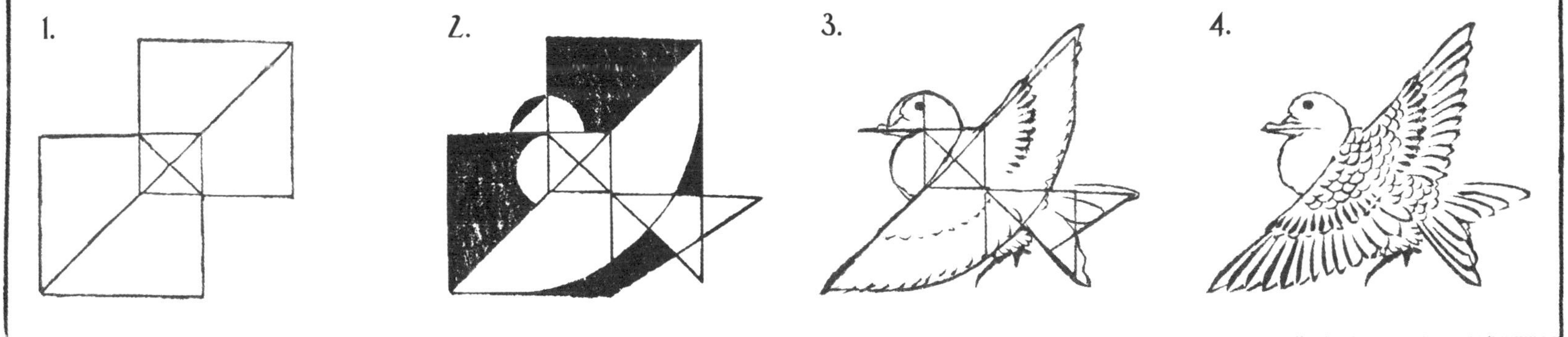

Hokusai used and repeated simple gestural marks,
to add a sense of movement to the water flowing
beneath this traditional-style bridge. The straight
line detail on the bridge contrasts with the curves
of the water, making the brickwork appear solid
in comparison. Hokusai shows how very simple
additions can be used to bring depth and dimension.

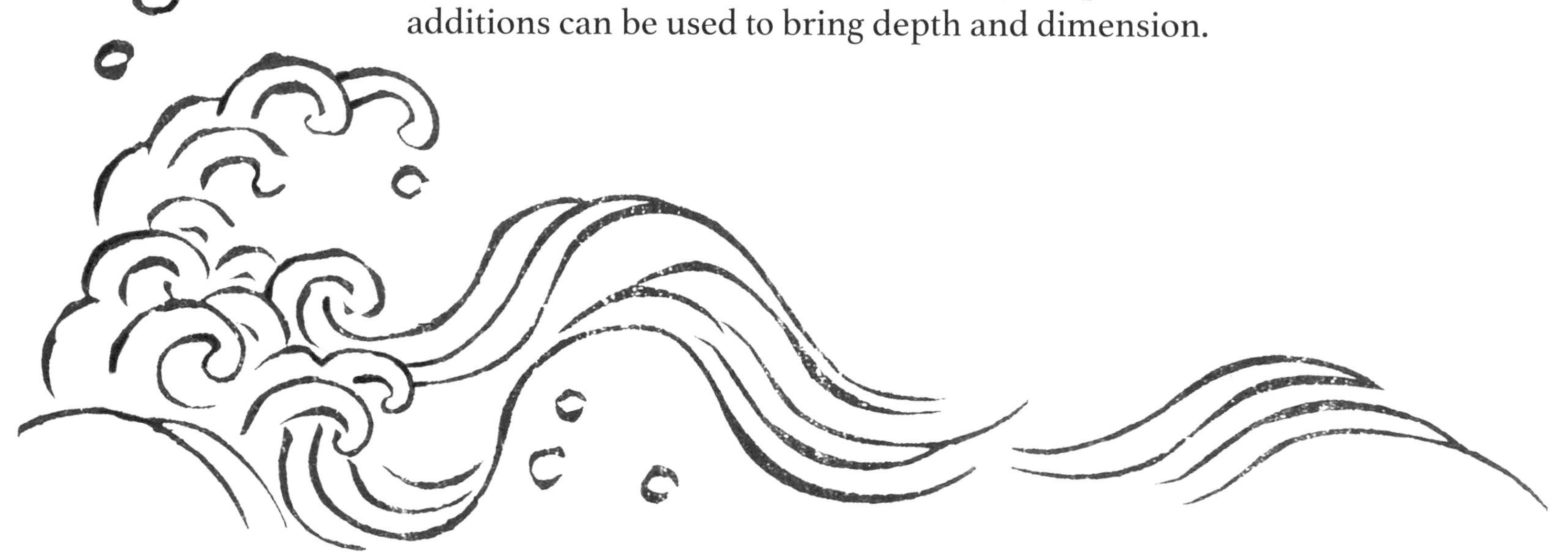

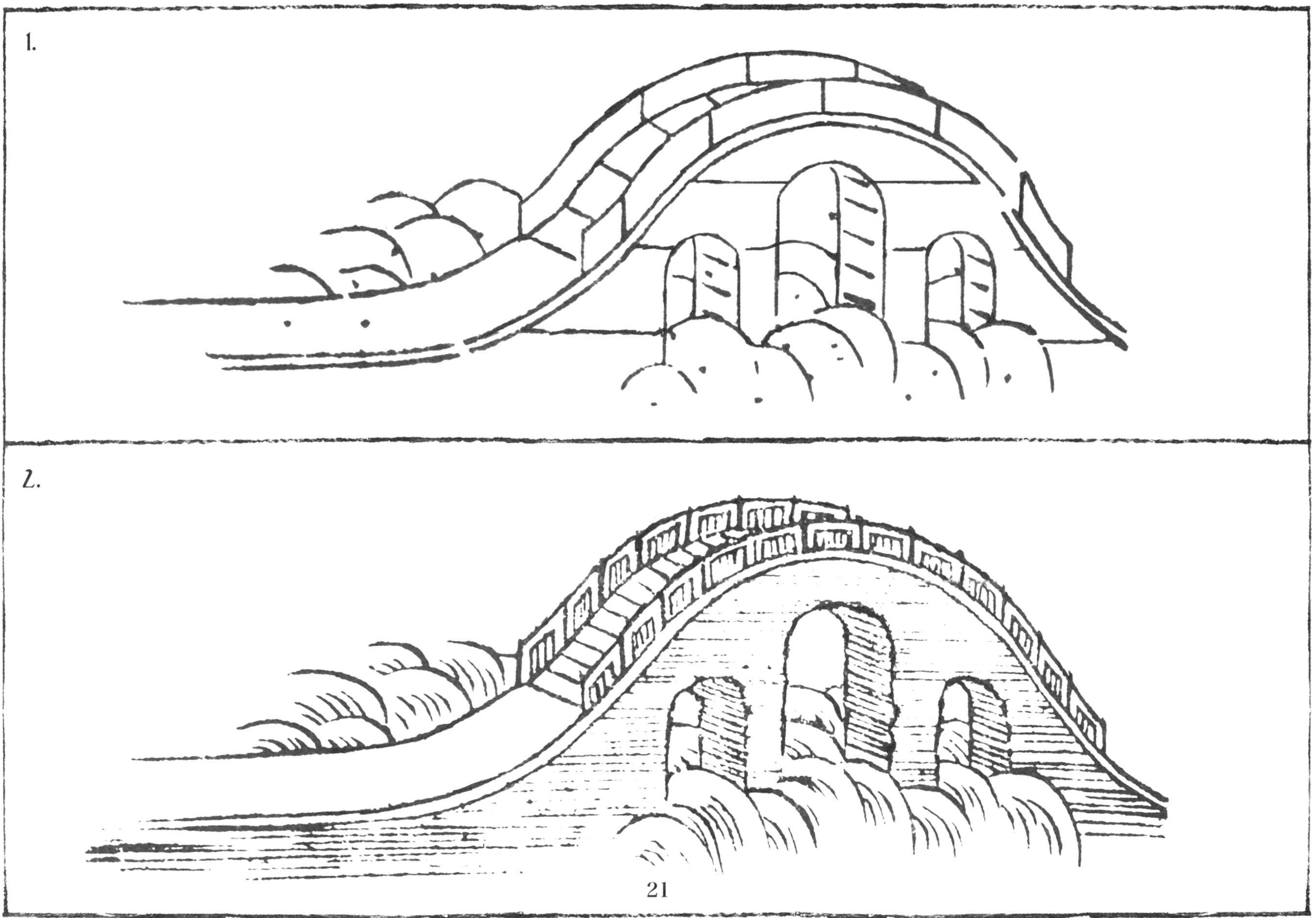
1.
2.

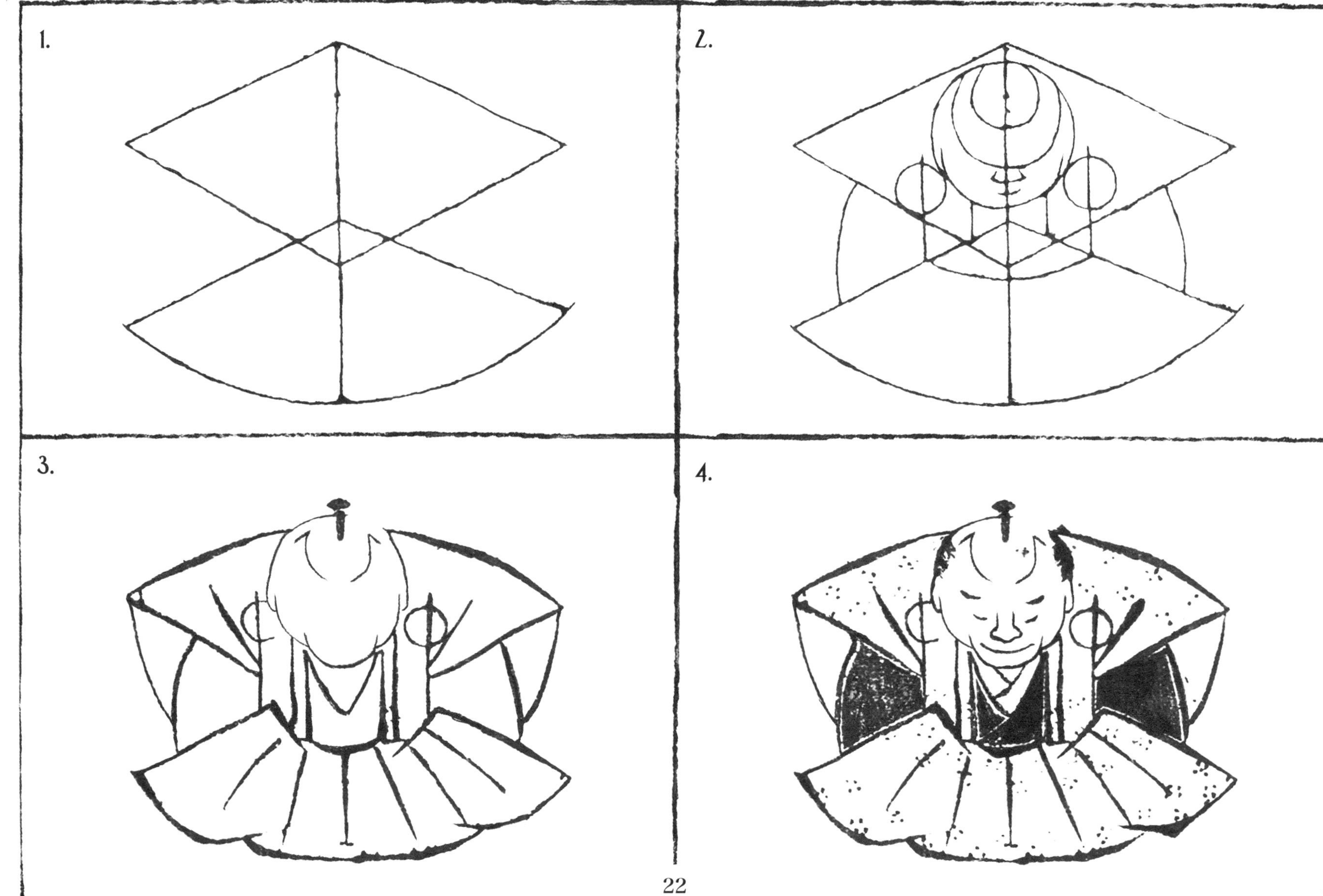

1.
2.
3.
4.

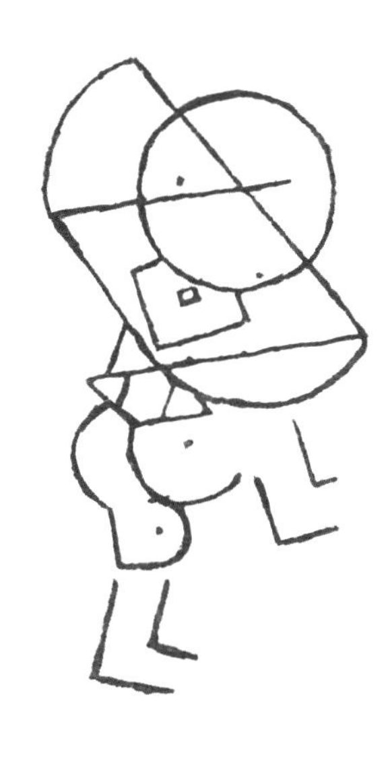
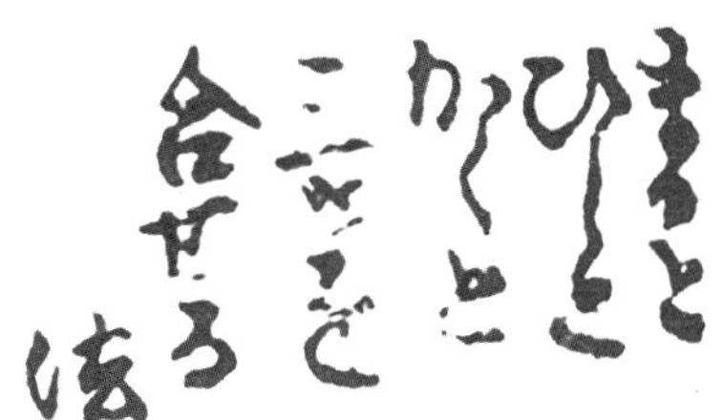

ほどと
ひくと
かくと
こゝをで
合せろ
法

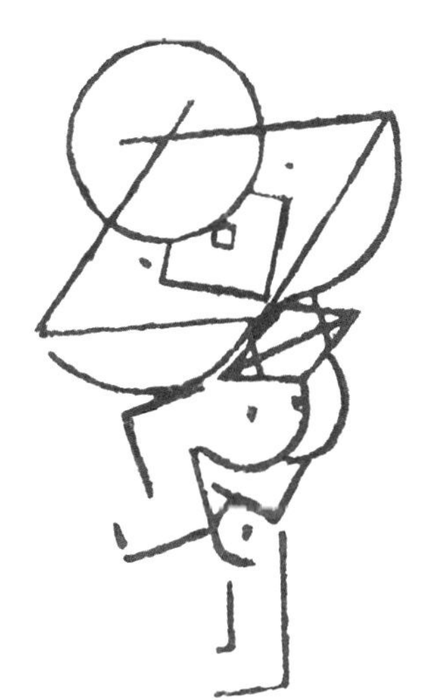
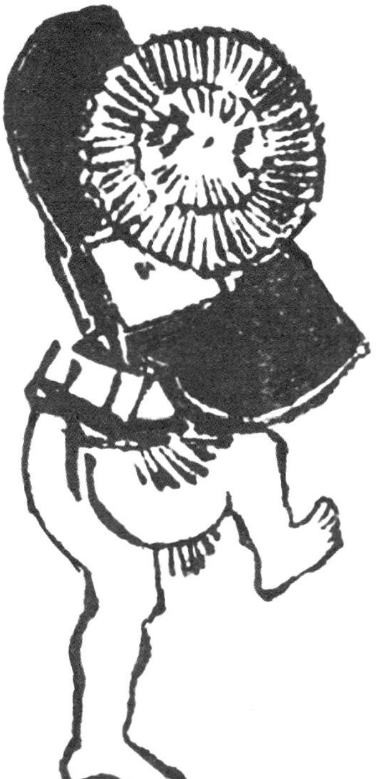
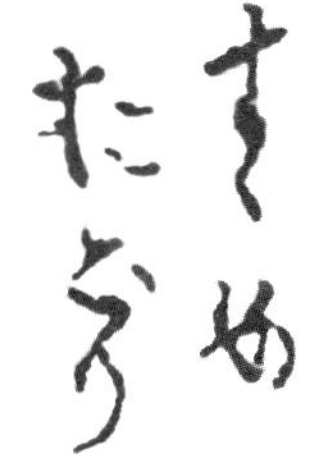

すゝめ
たらり

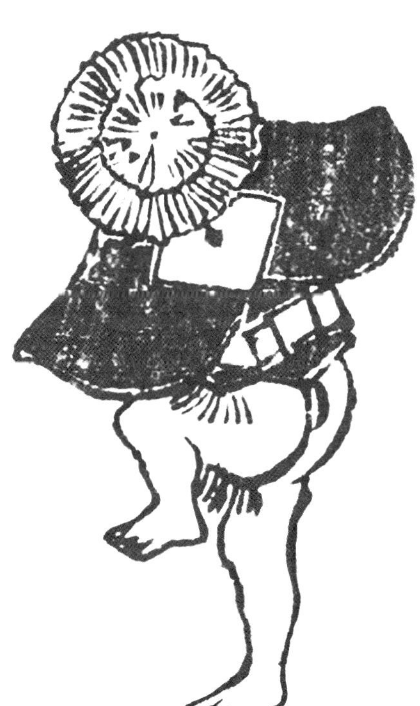
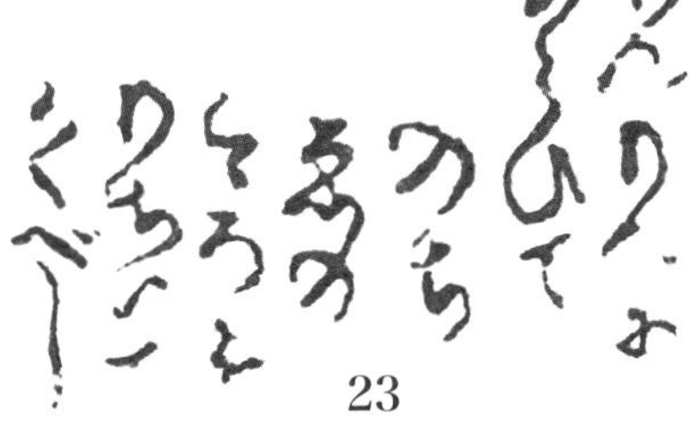

わたりゝよ
あくのて
のち
ある
ところ
わろを
りちに
くべ―

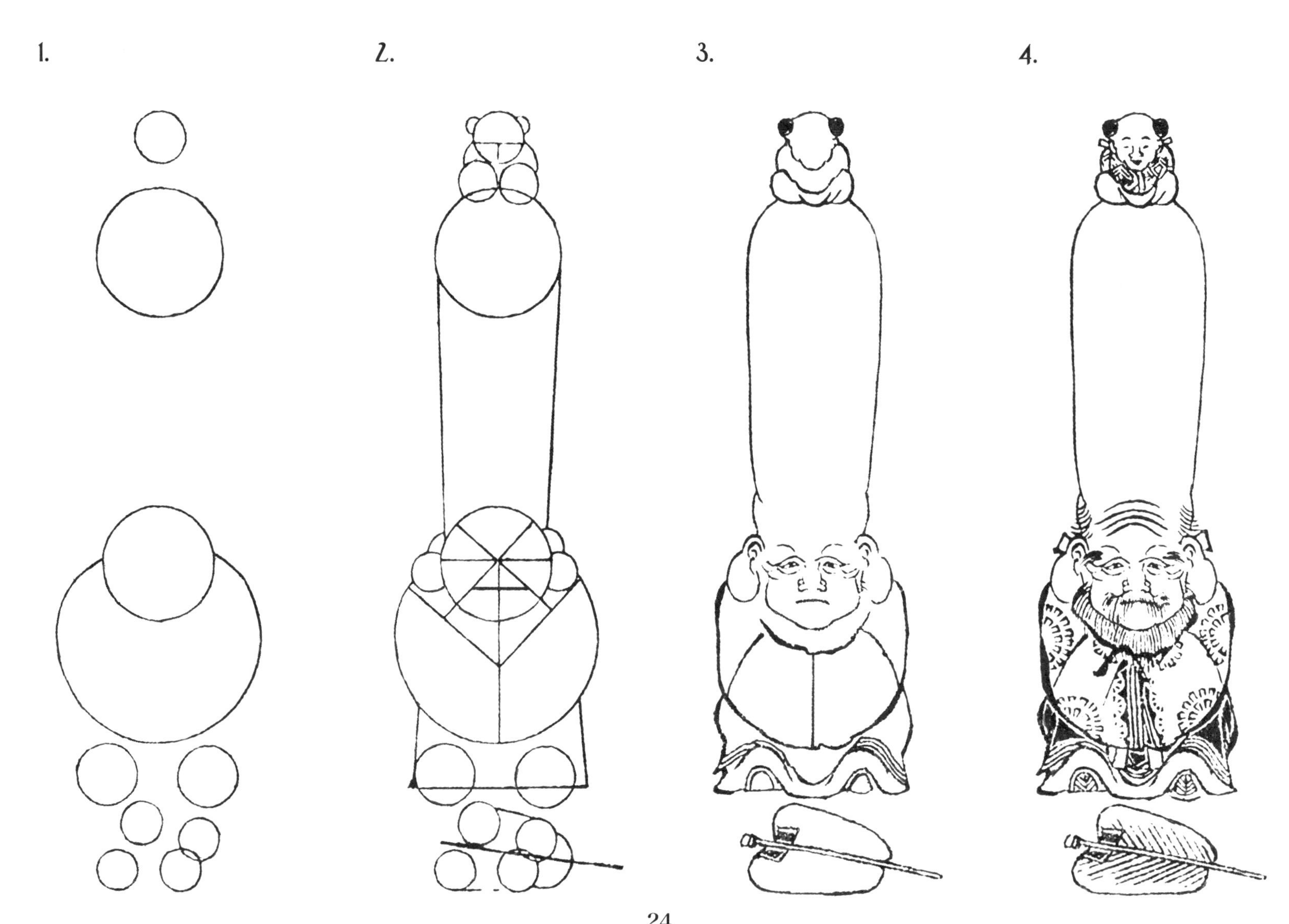

1.
2.
3.
4.
24

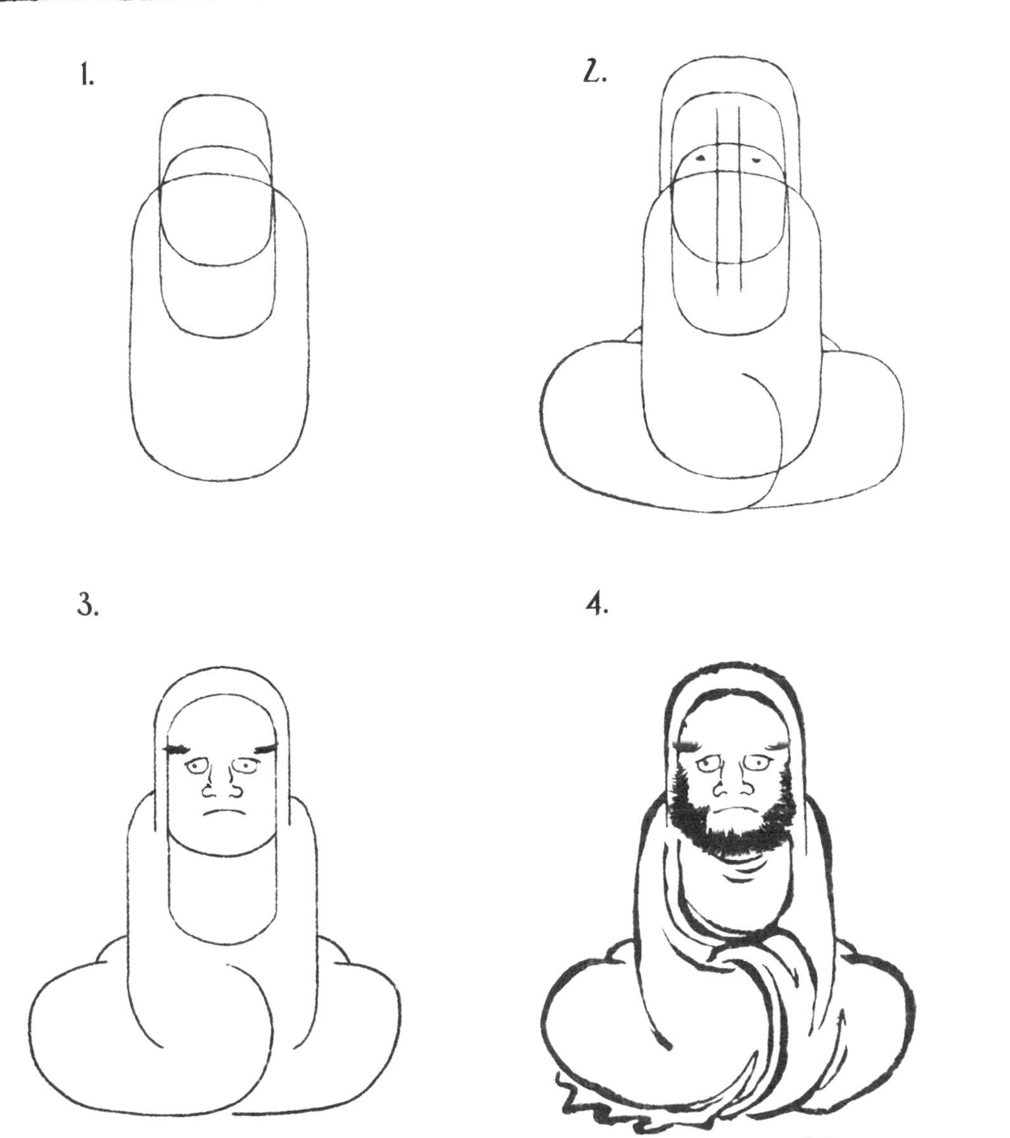

Hokusai's figures can often be broken down into simple curves and circles, which can then be connected to slowly reveal the intended form.

25

1. 
2. 
3.

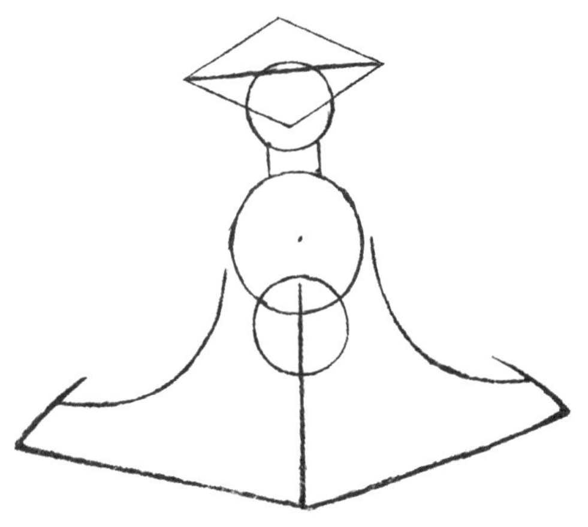

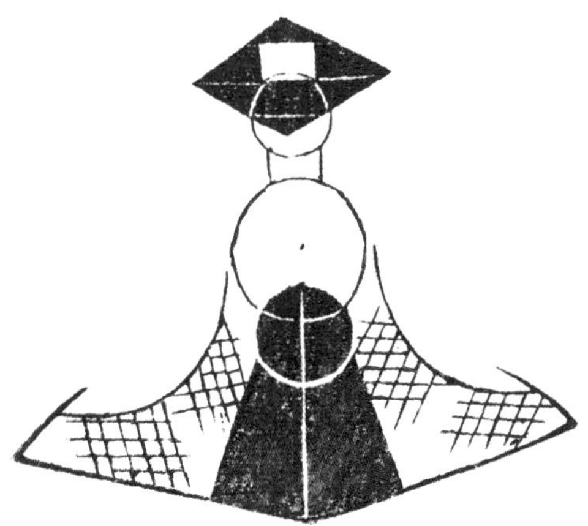

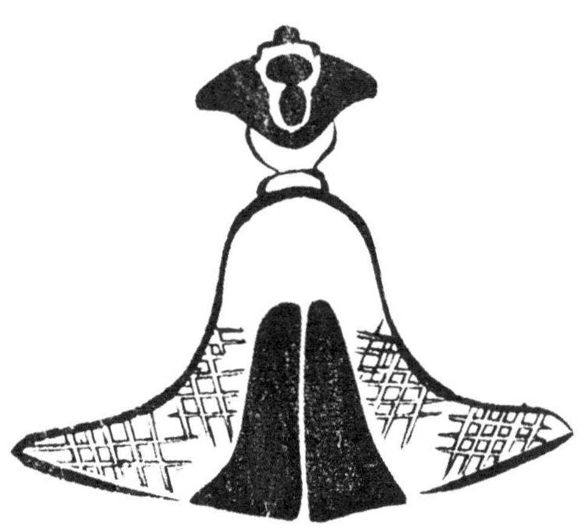

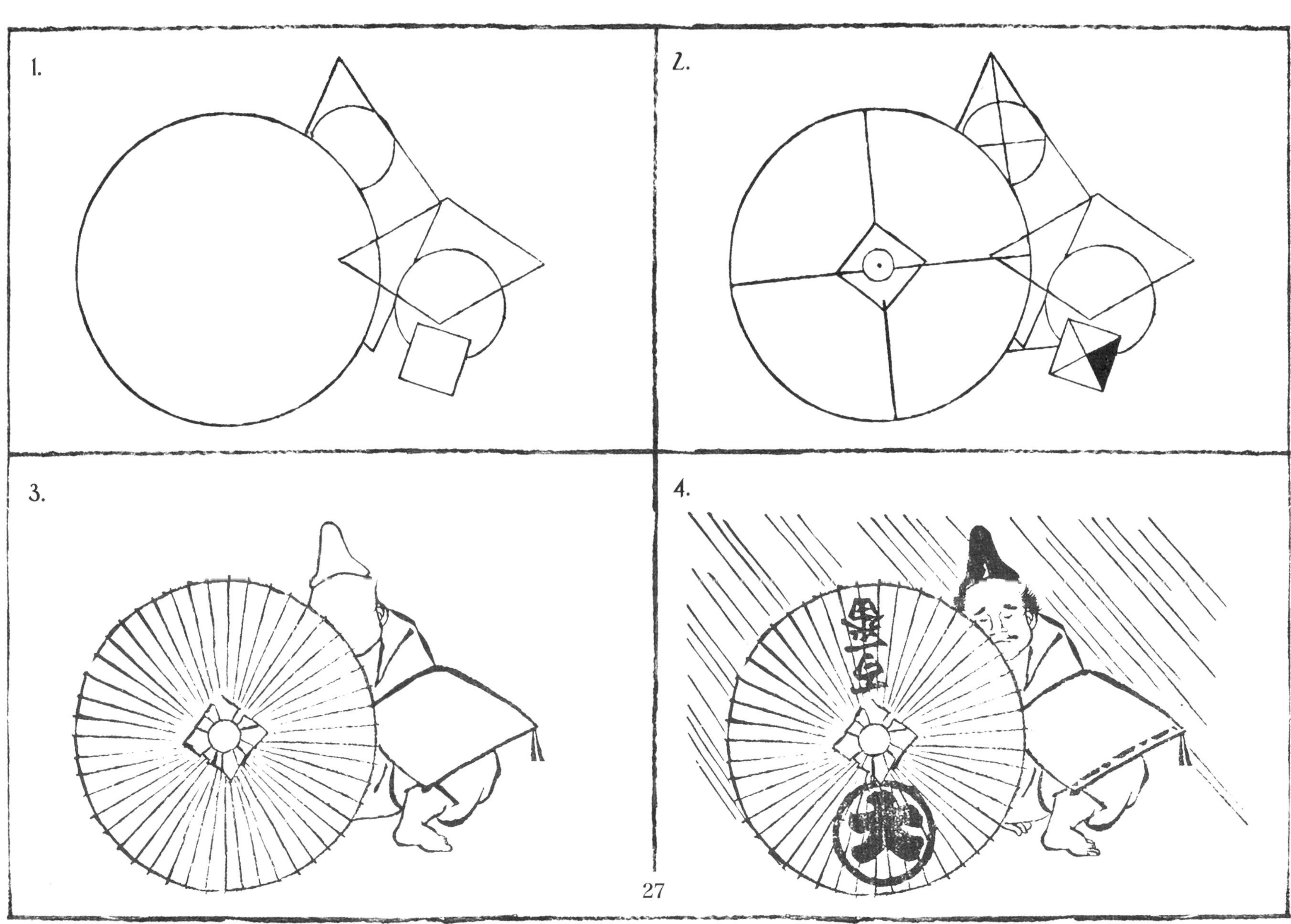

1.
2.
3.
4.

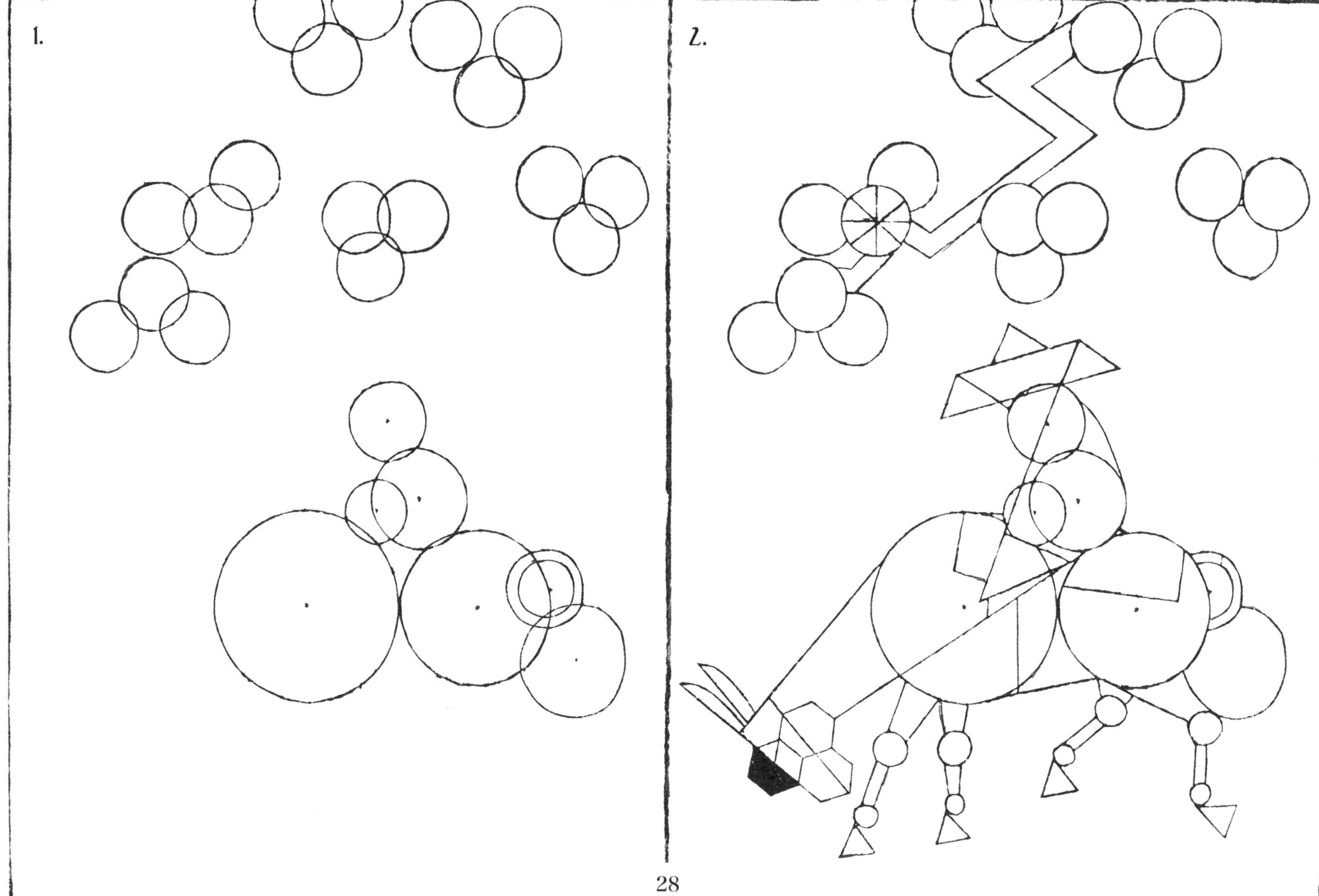

1.
2.

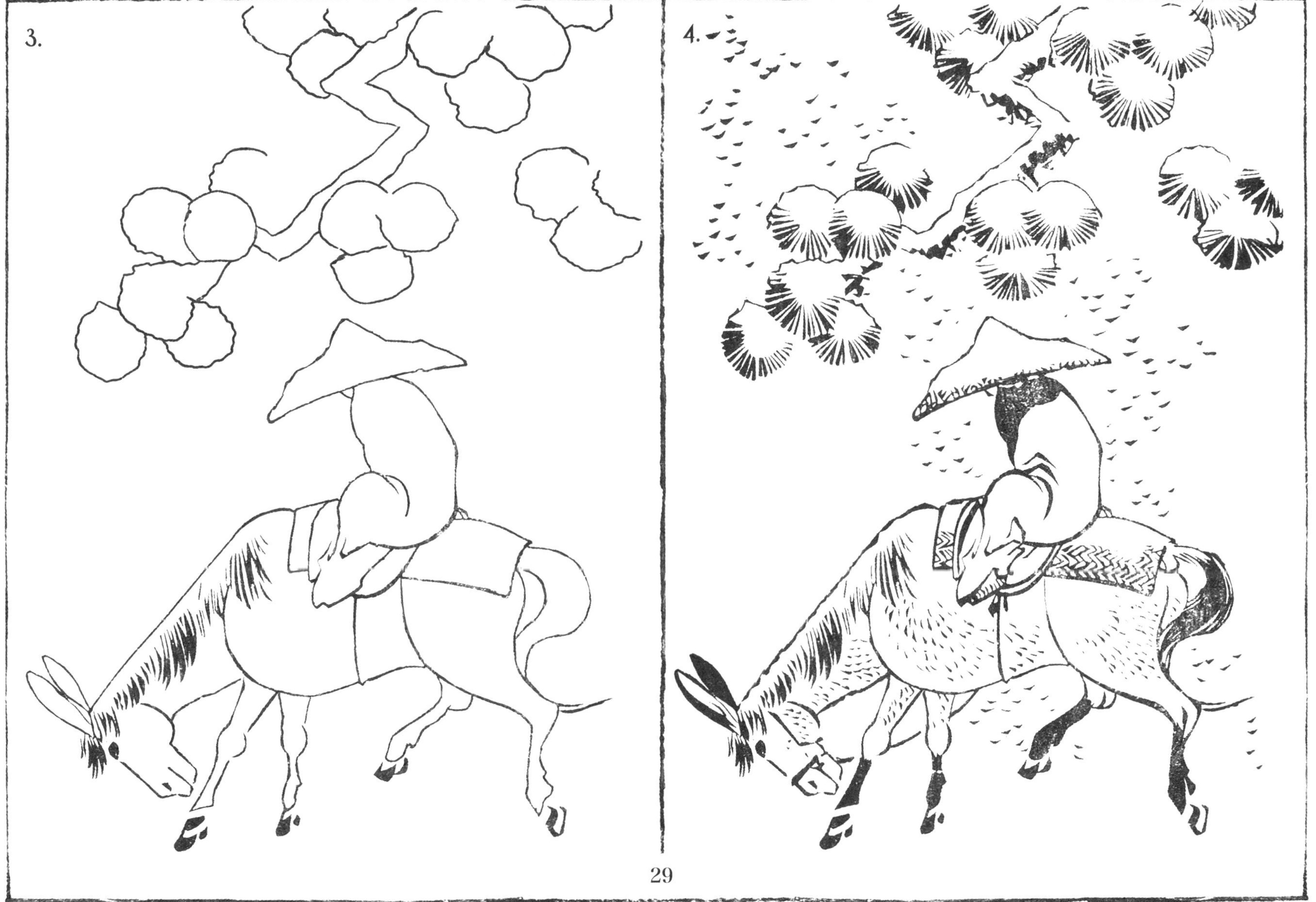

3.
4.

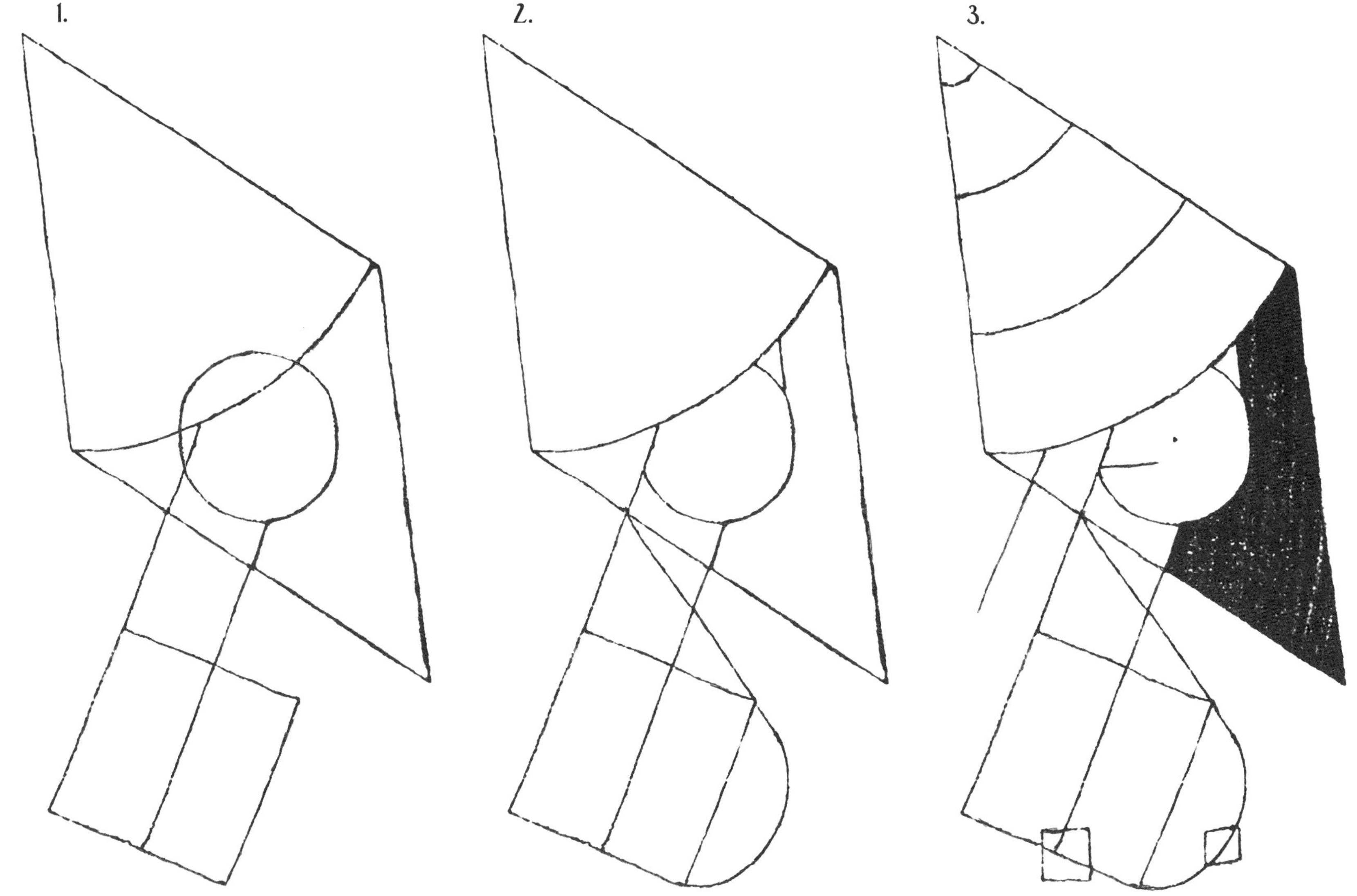

1.
2.
3.

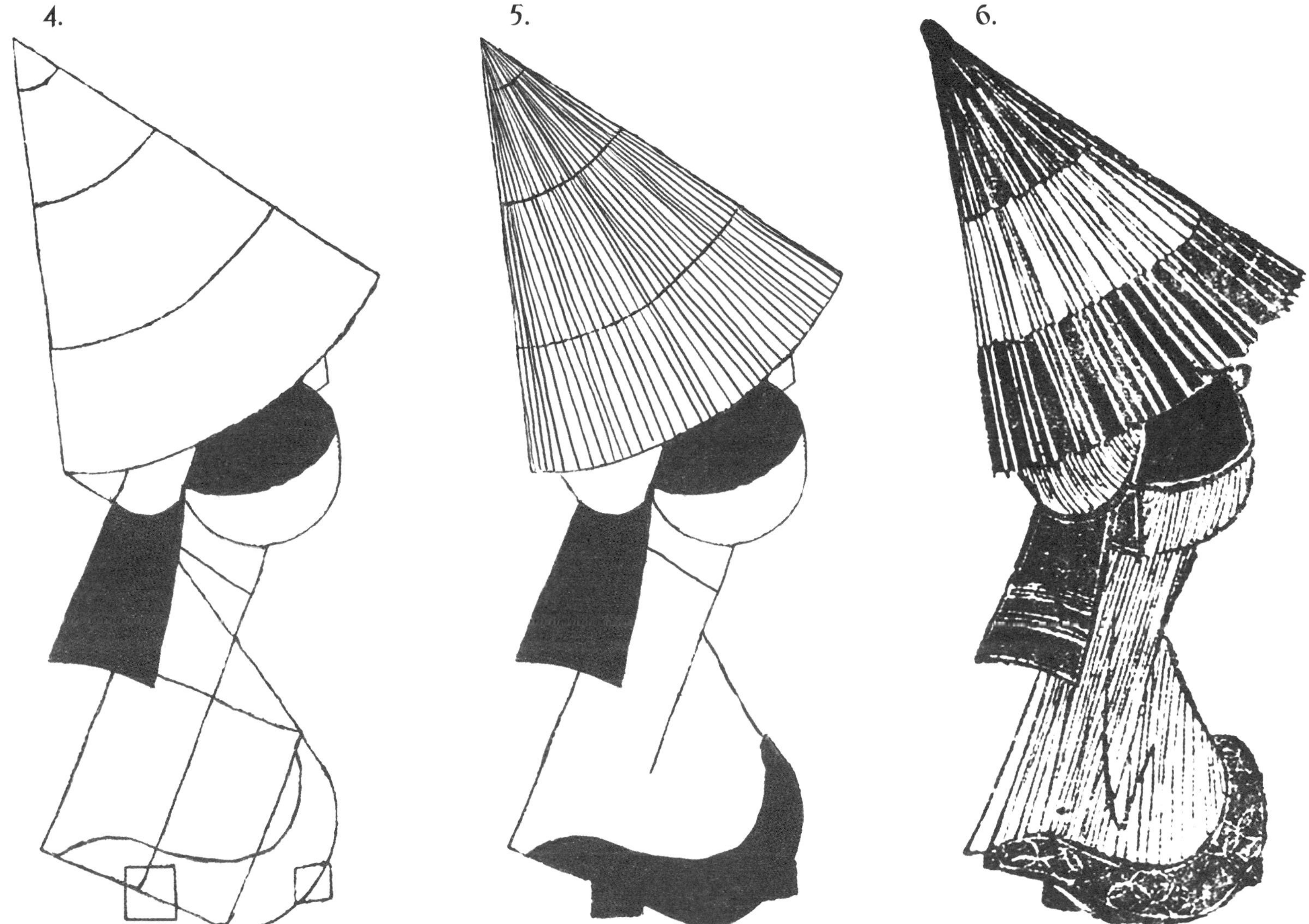

4.
5.
6.

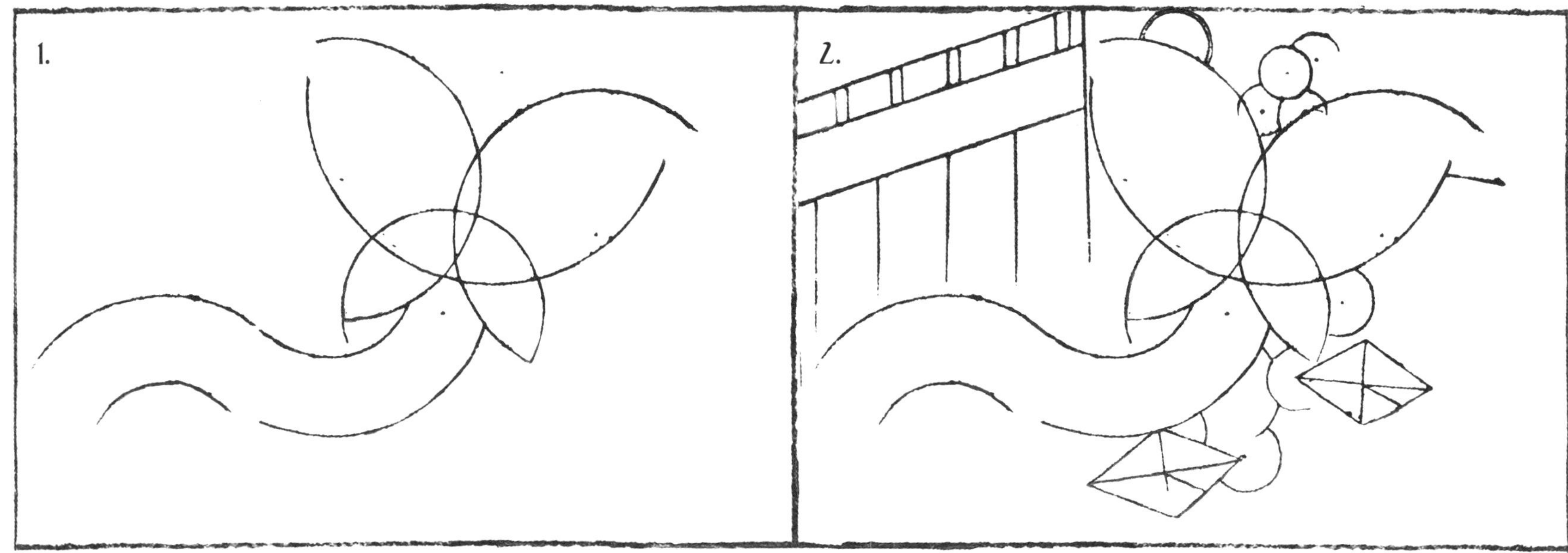

1.
2.

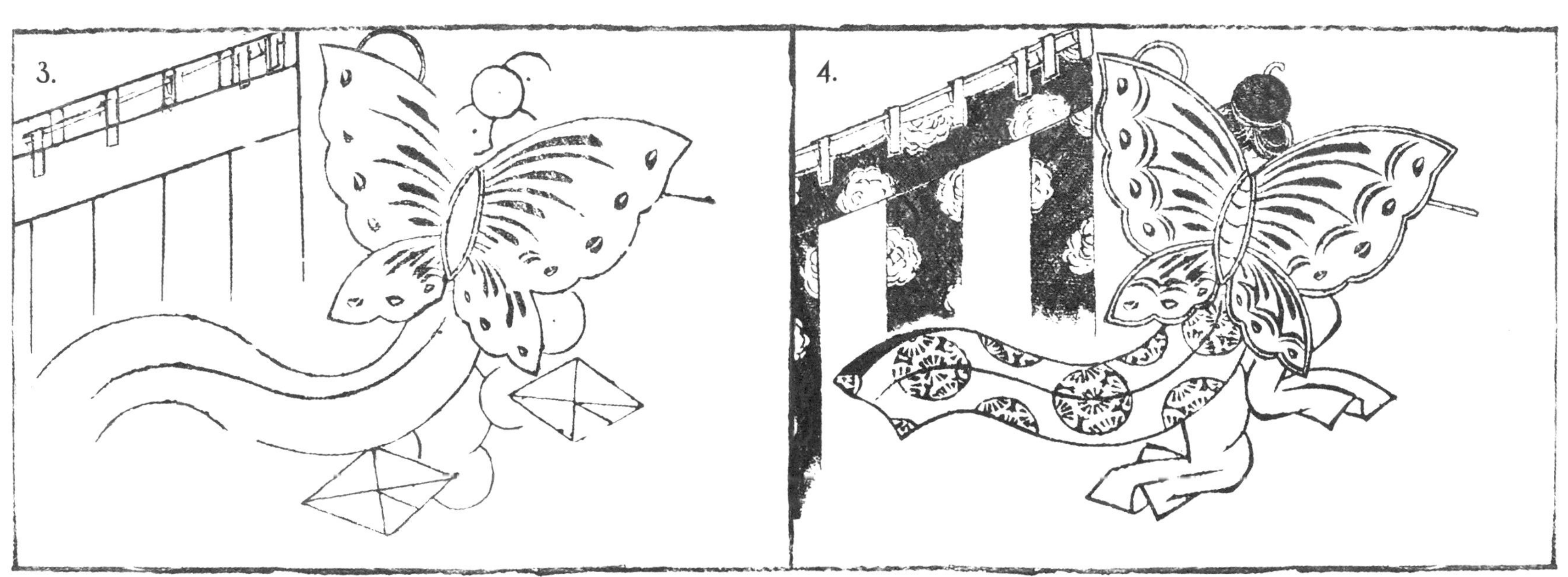

3.
4.

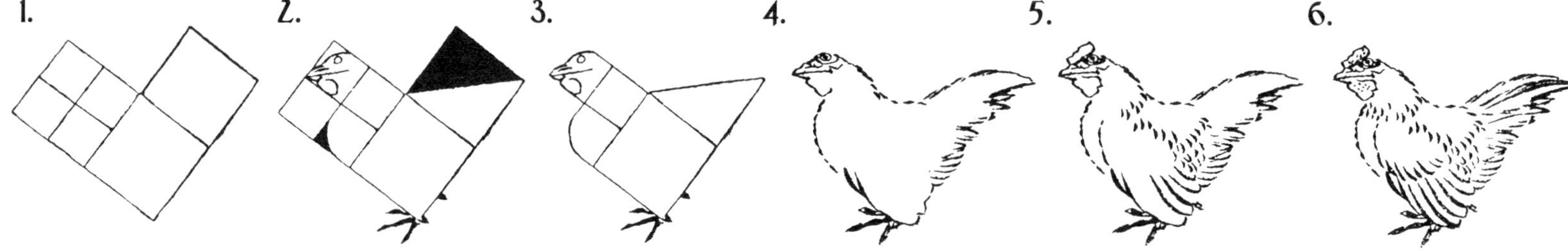

1.
2.
3.
4.
5.
6.

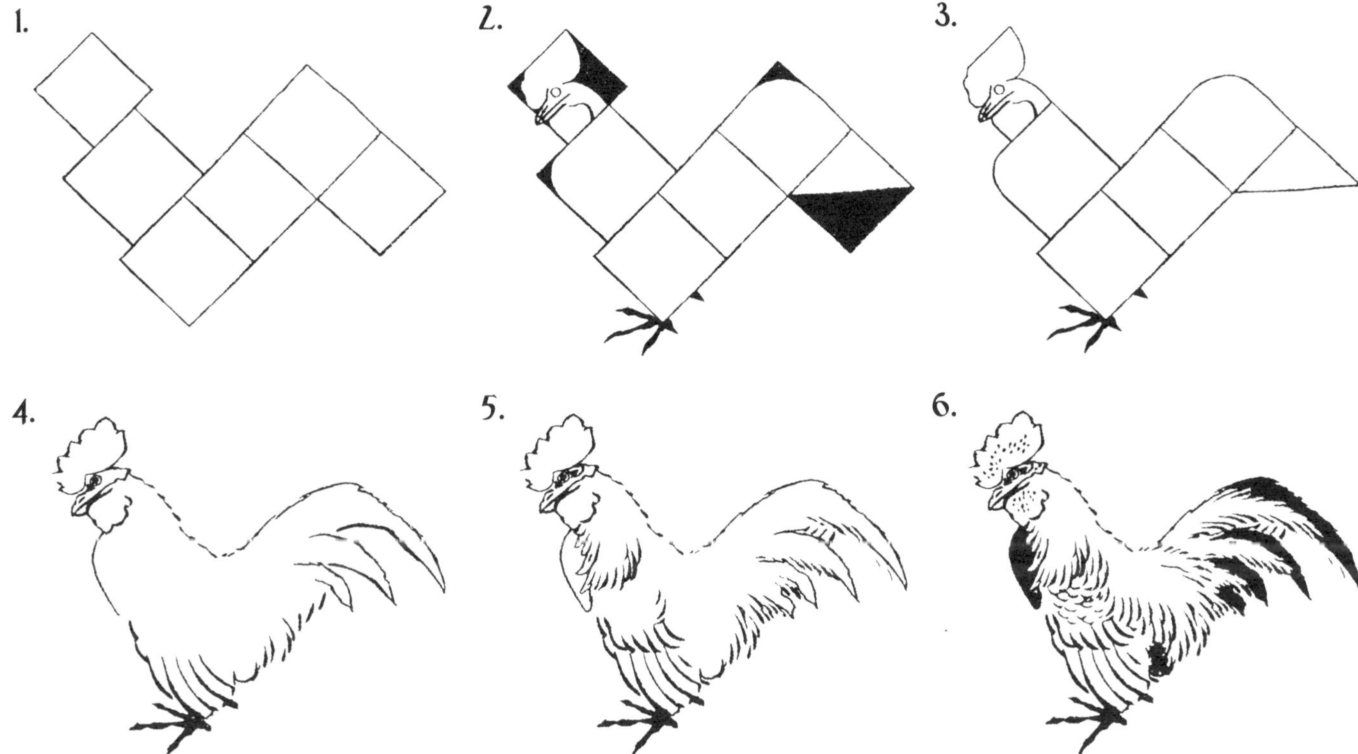

1.
2.
3.
4.
5.
6.

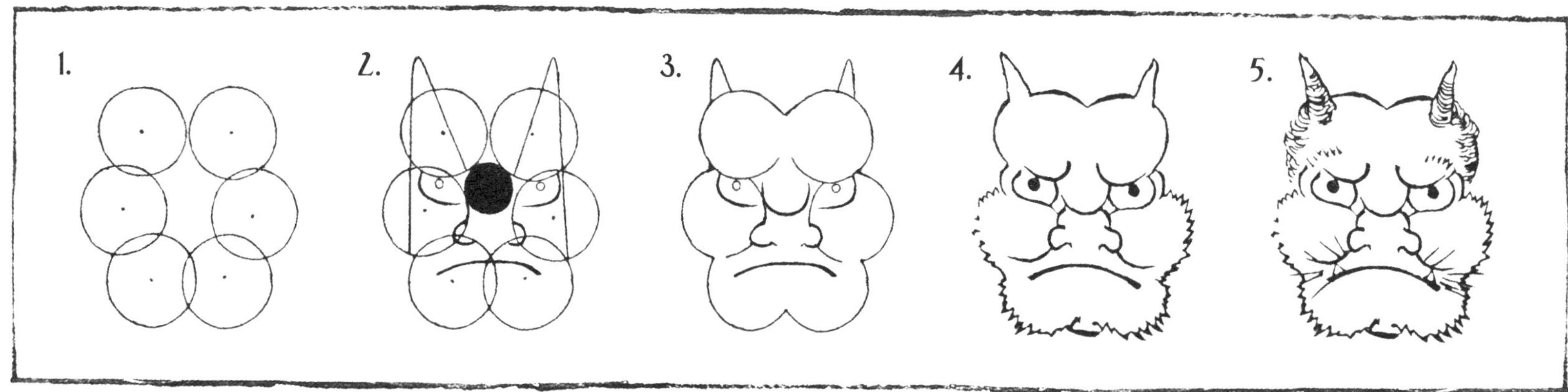

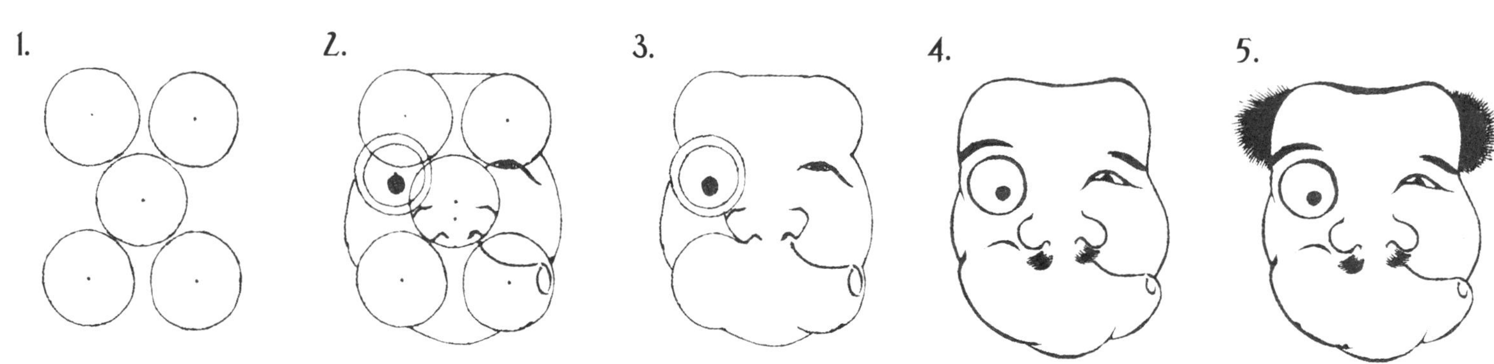

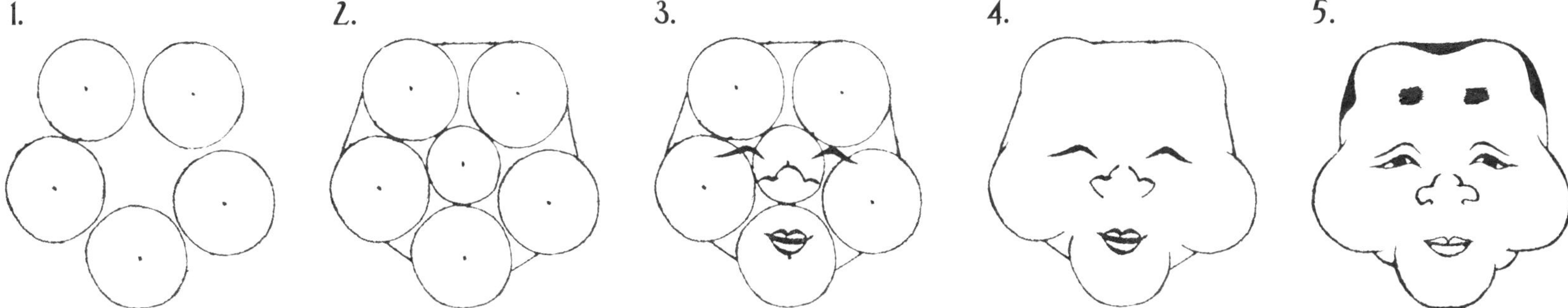

1.
2.
3.
4.
5.

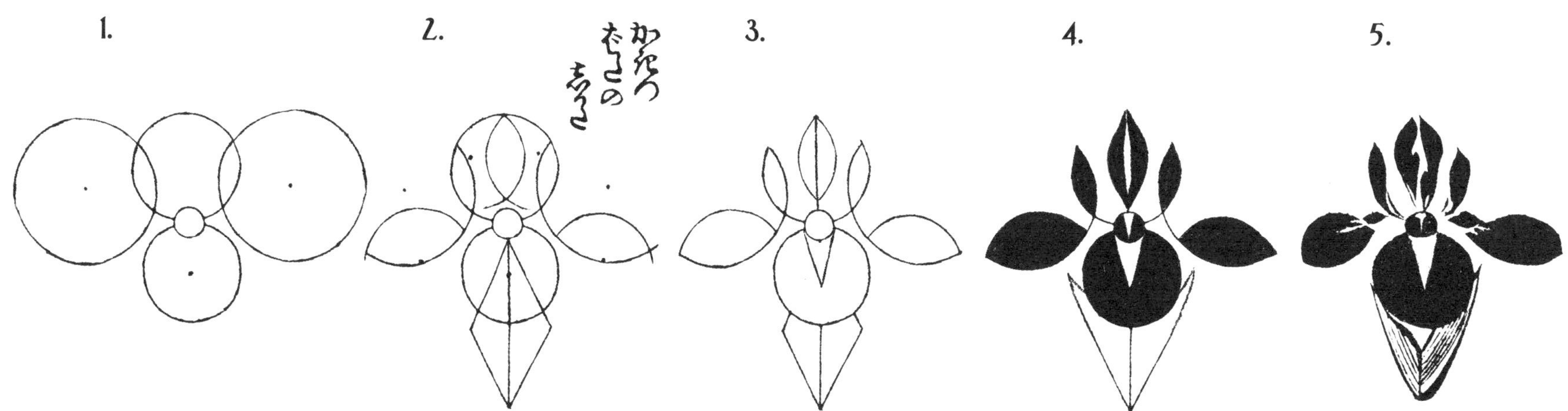

1.
2.
3.
4.
5.
かきつ
ばたの
はな

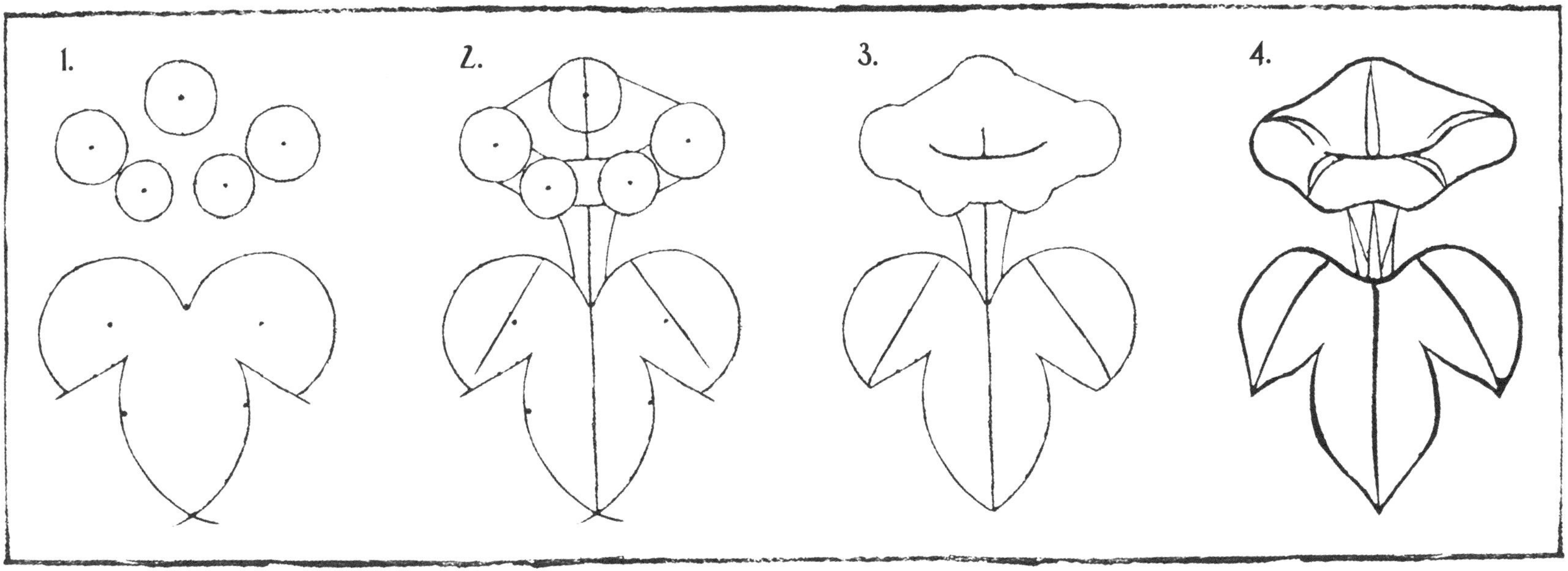

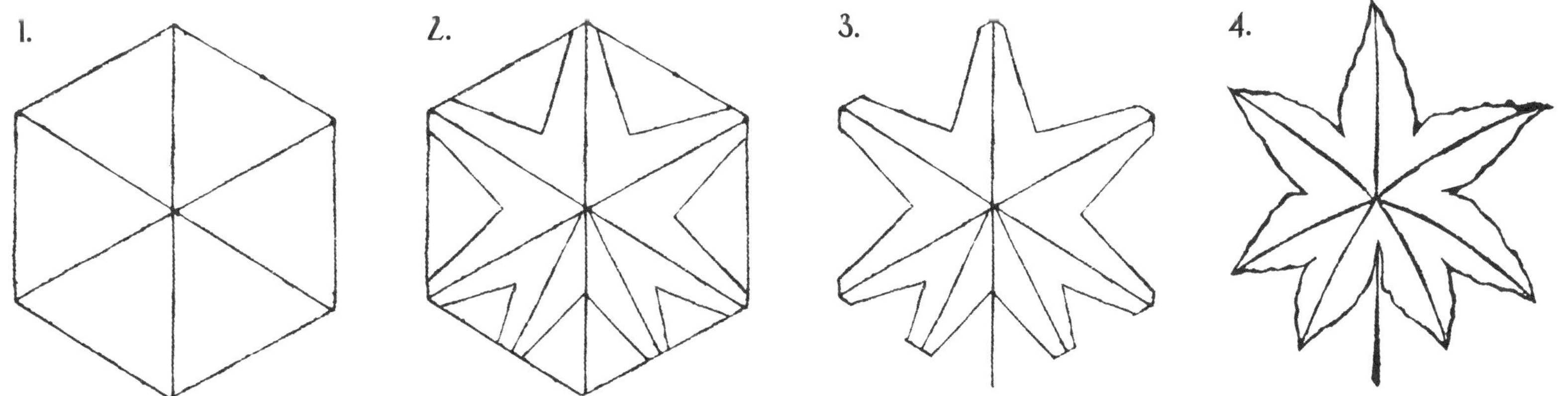

1.
2.
3.
4.
1.
2.
3.
4.

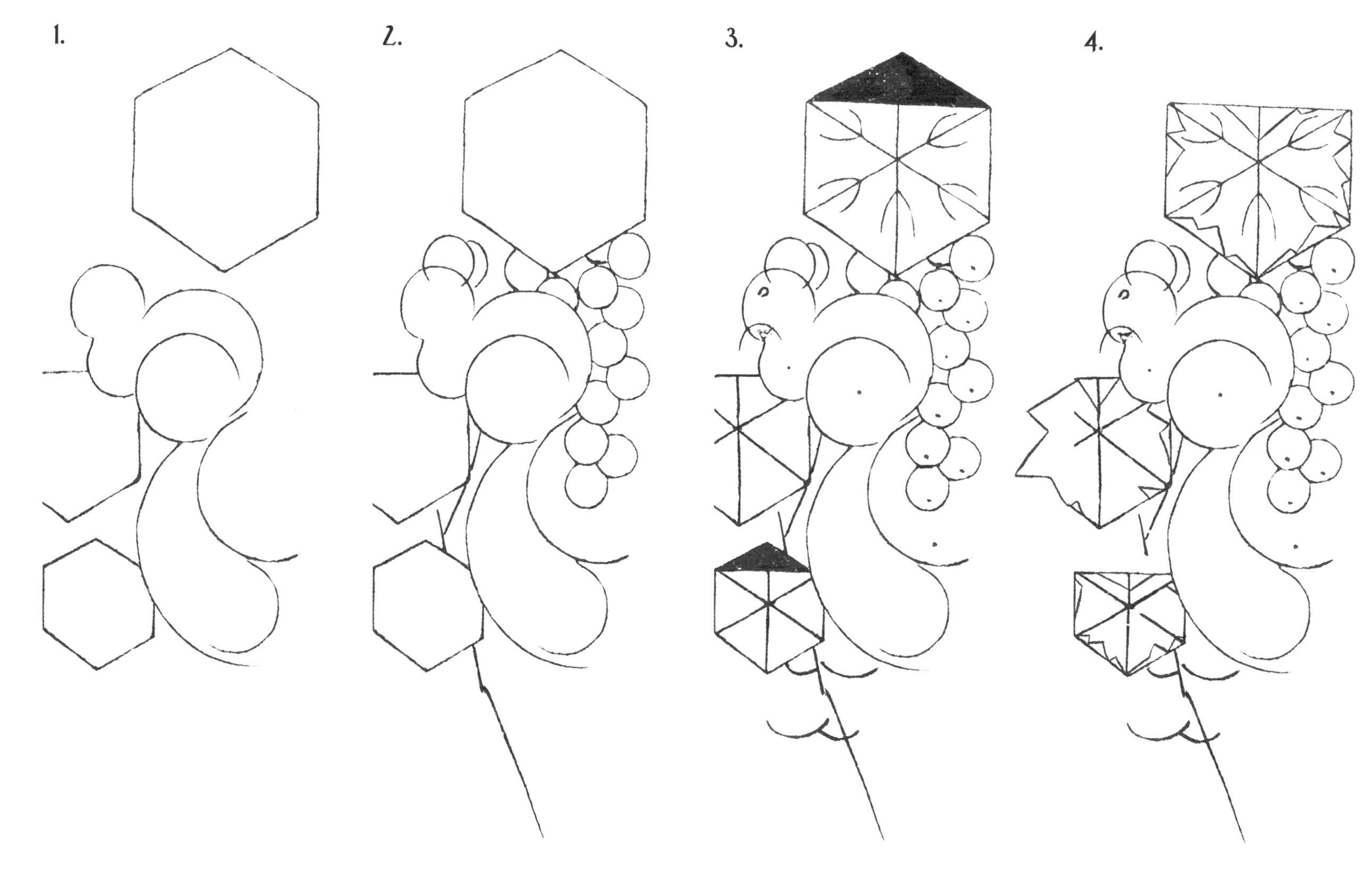

1.
2.
3.
4.

5.

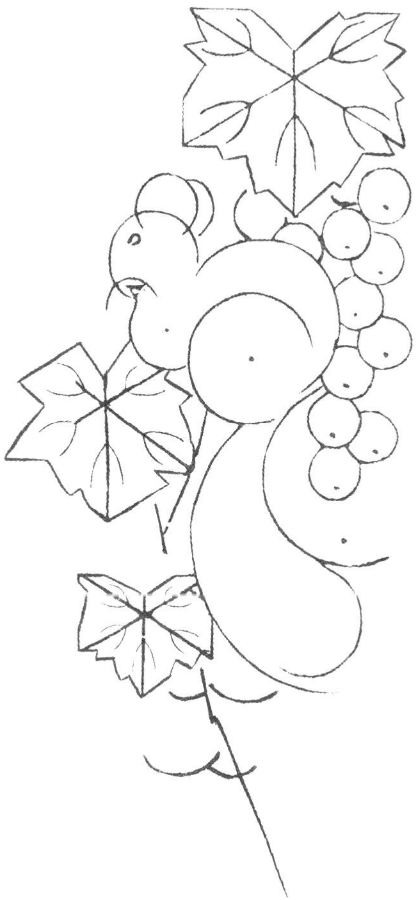

6.

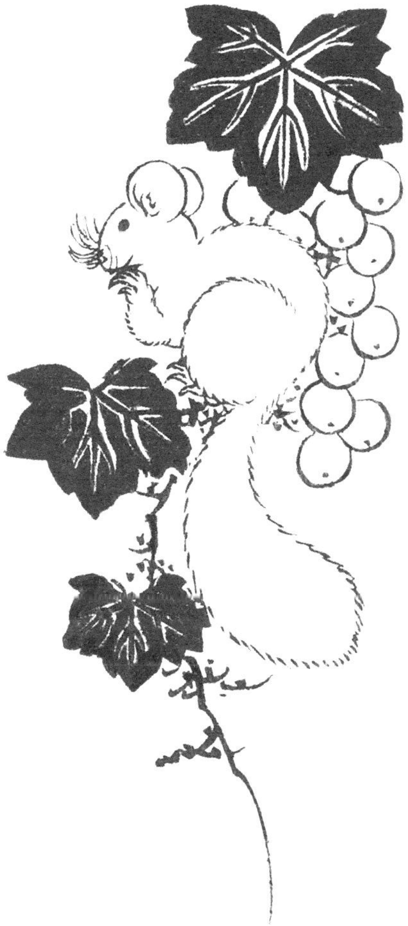

Notice in this example how shapes can be used to create not just the subject, but the spaces around it. In Step 1, a partial circle is drawn to map out the the area around the back of the squirrel's tail.

1.

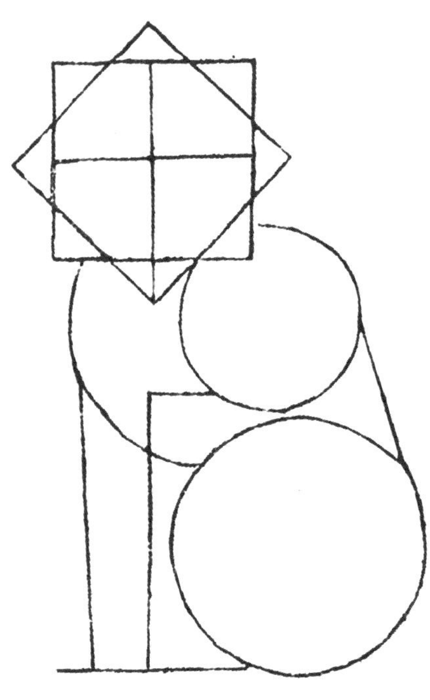

2.

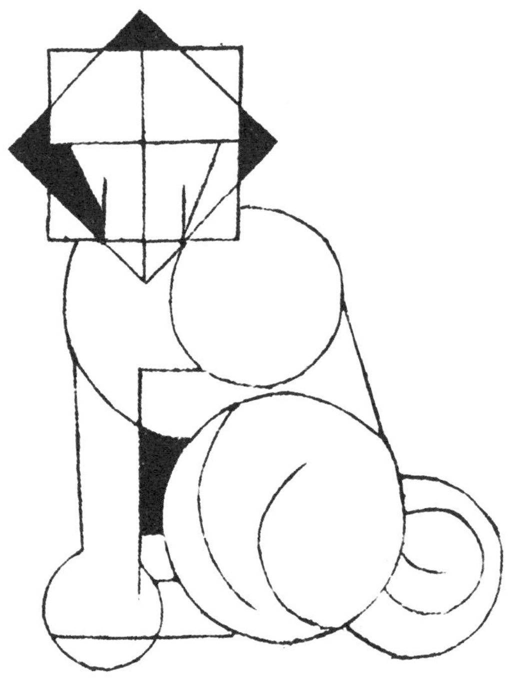

3.

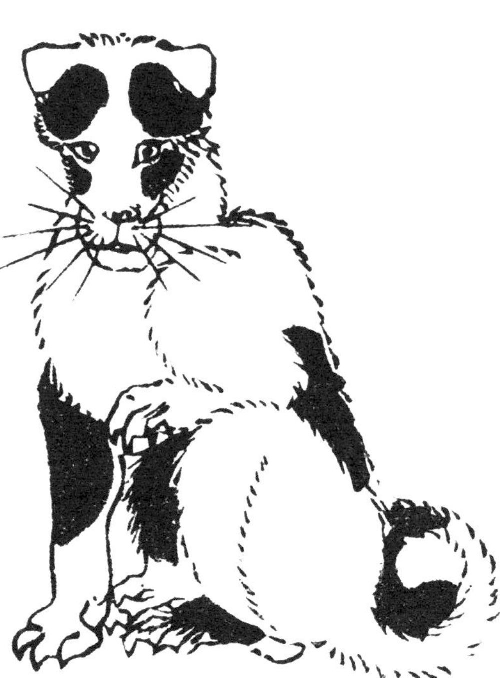

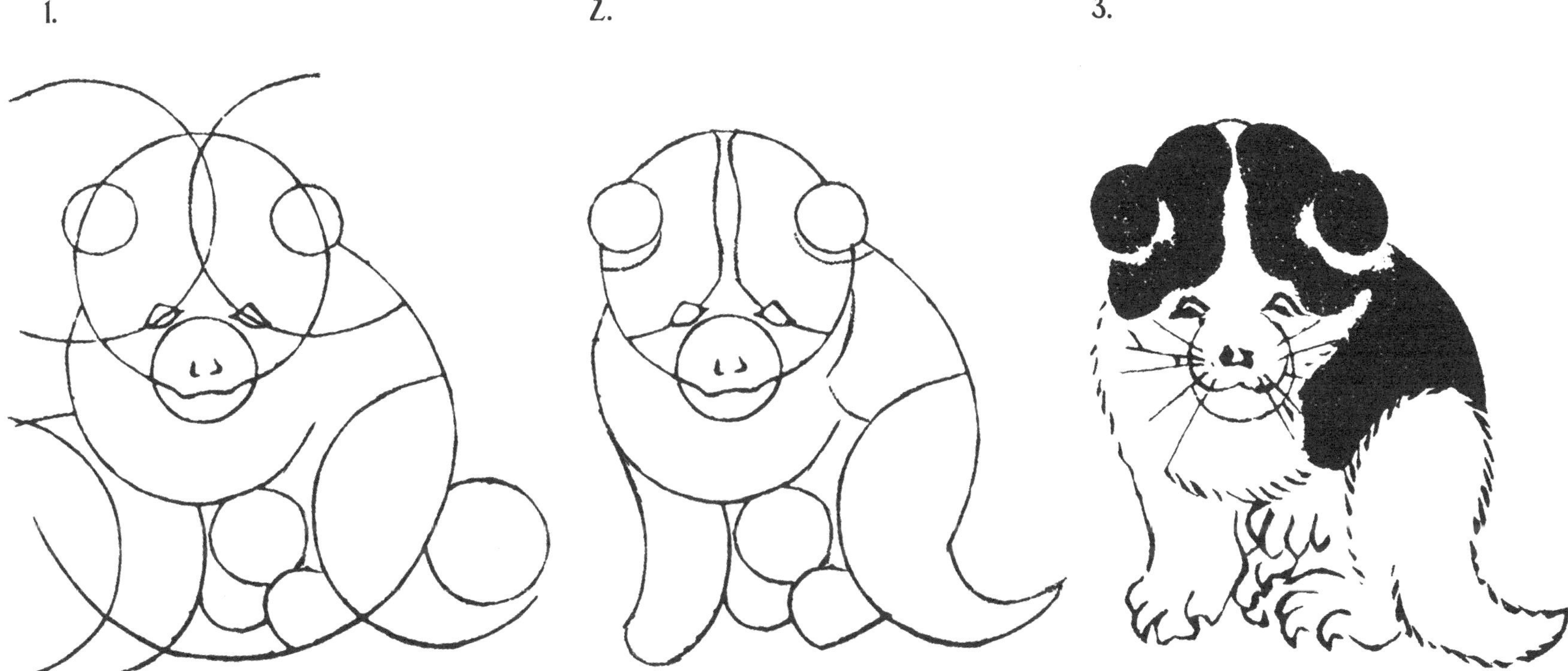

1.
2.
3.

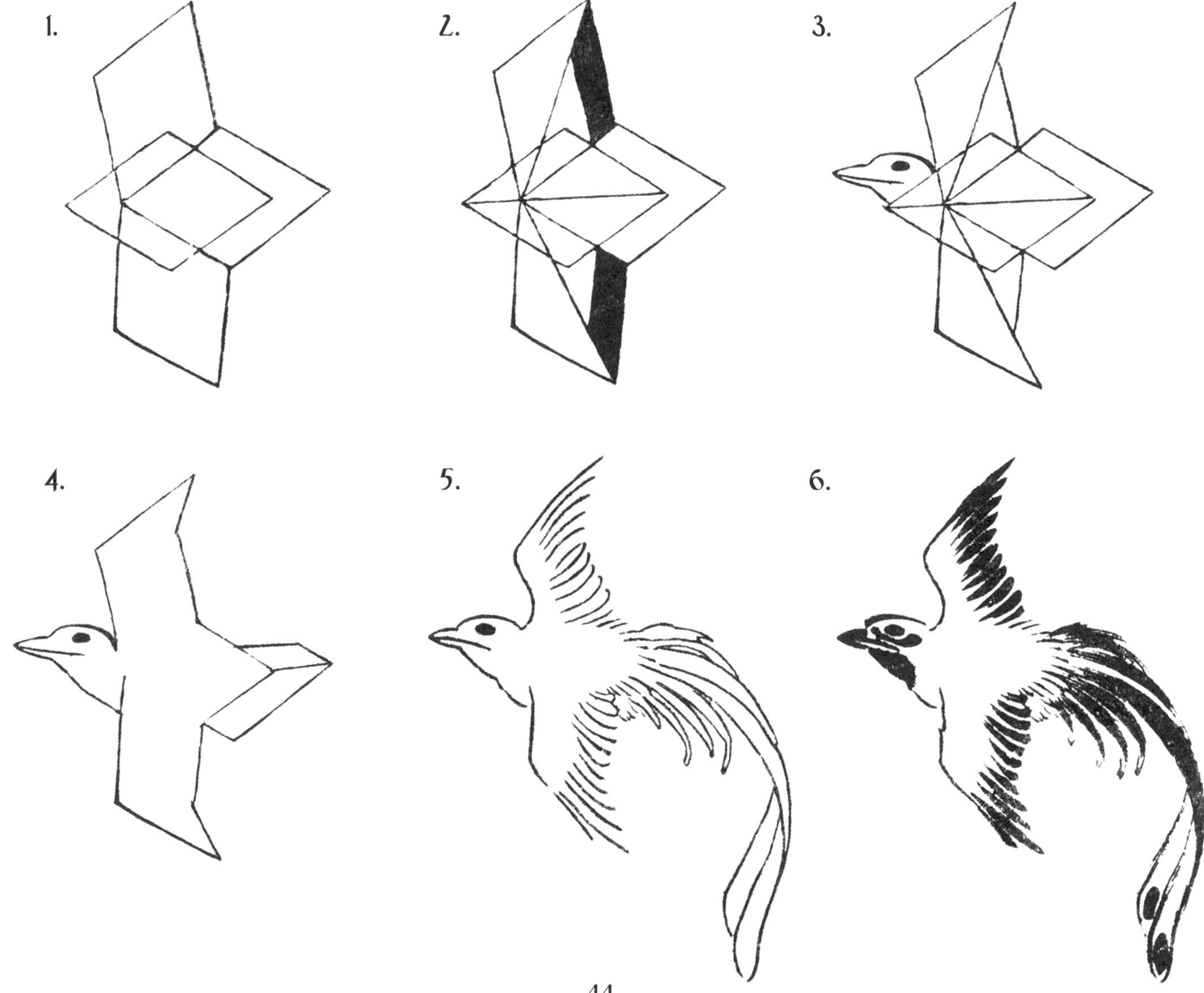

1.
2.
3.
4.
5.
6.

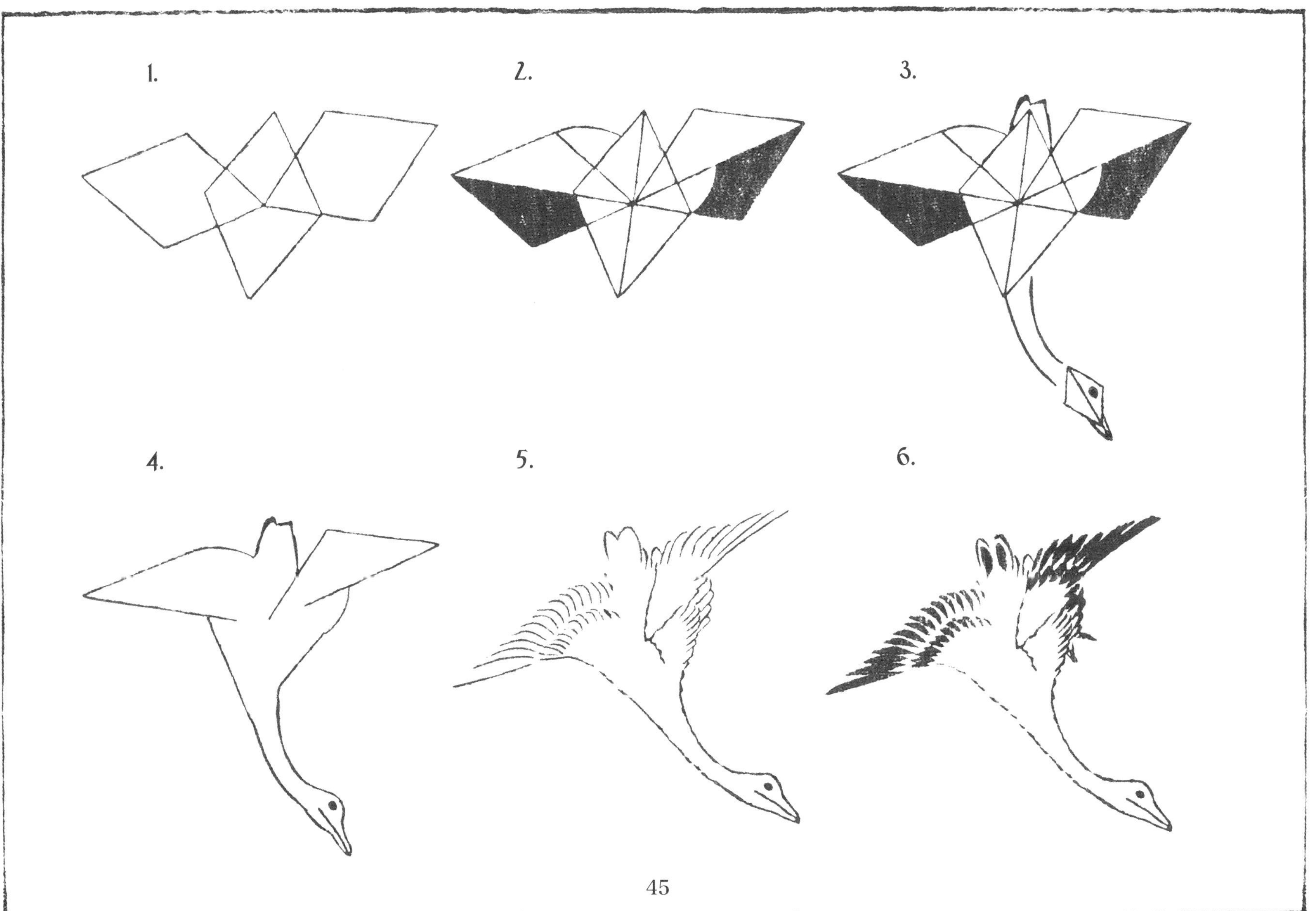

1.
2.
3.
4.
5.
6.

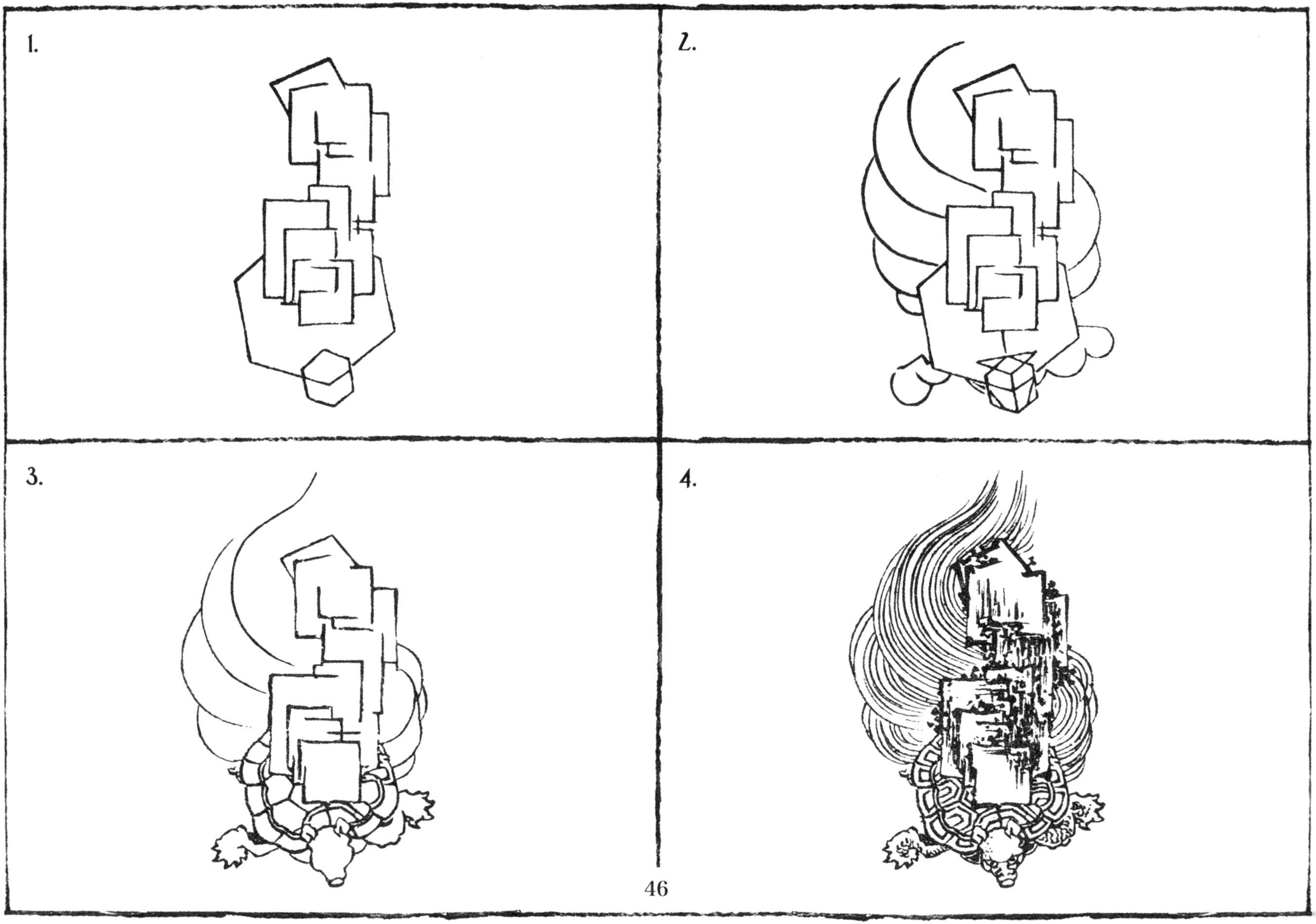

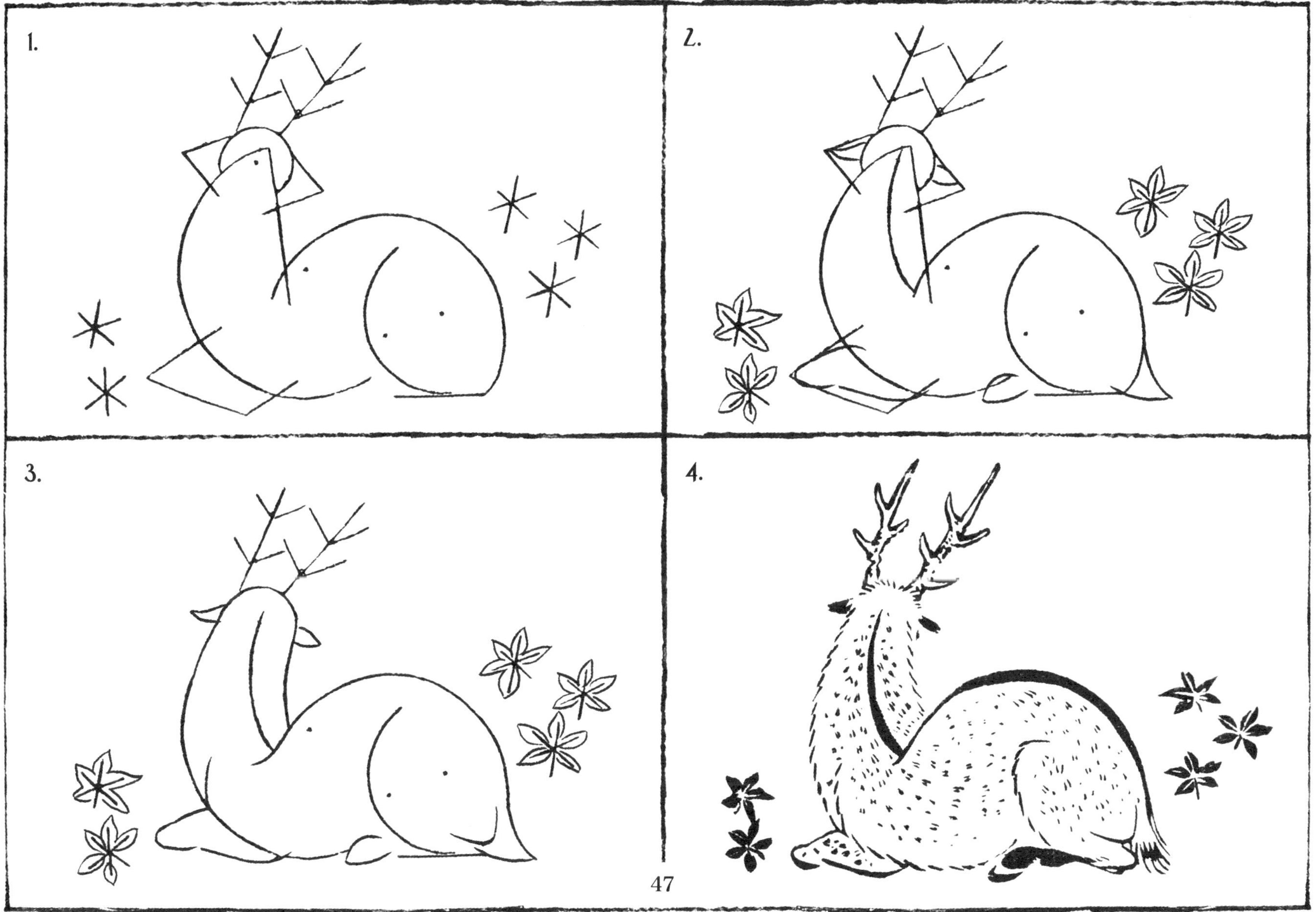

1.
2.
3.
4.

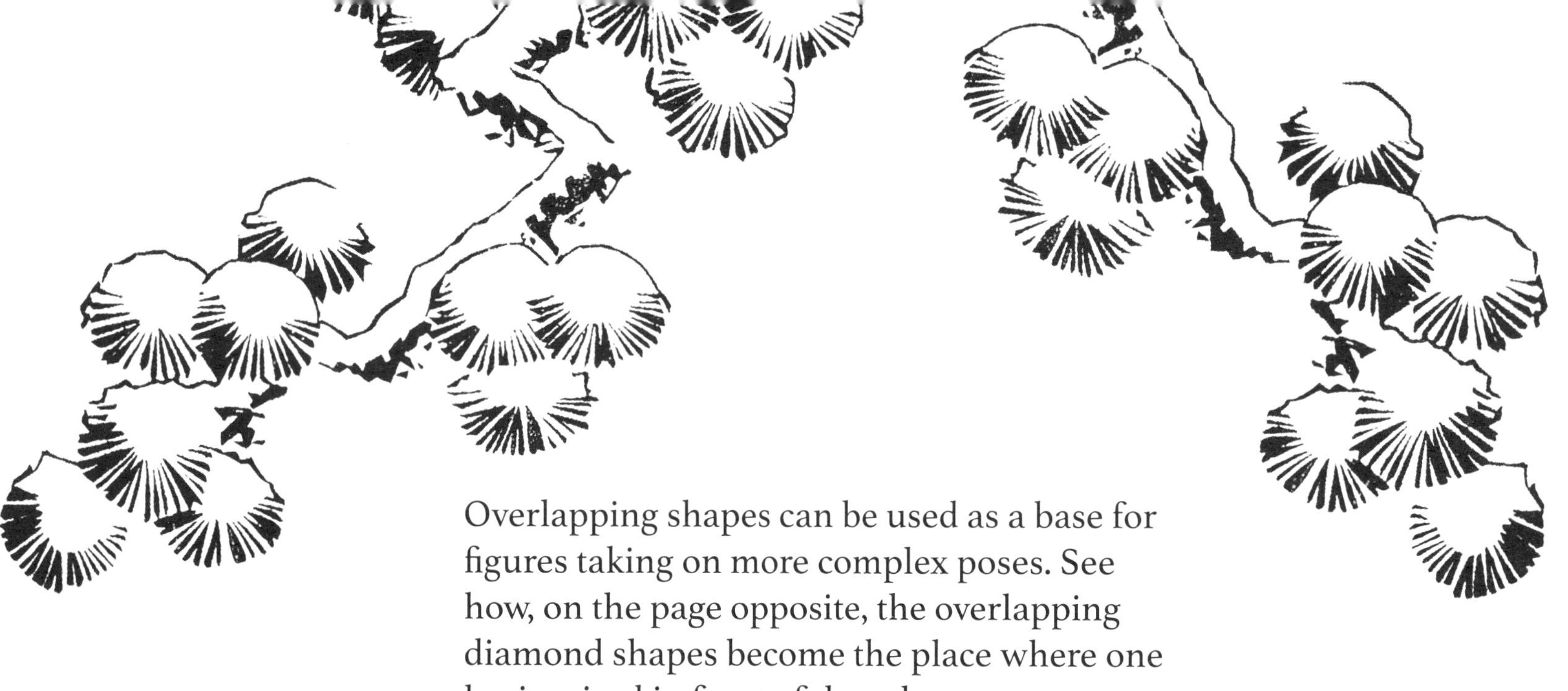

Overlapping shapes can be used as a base for figures taking on more complex poses. See how, on the page opposite, the overlapping diamond shapes become the place where one leg is raised in front of the other.

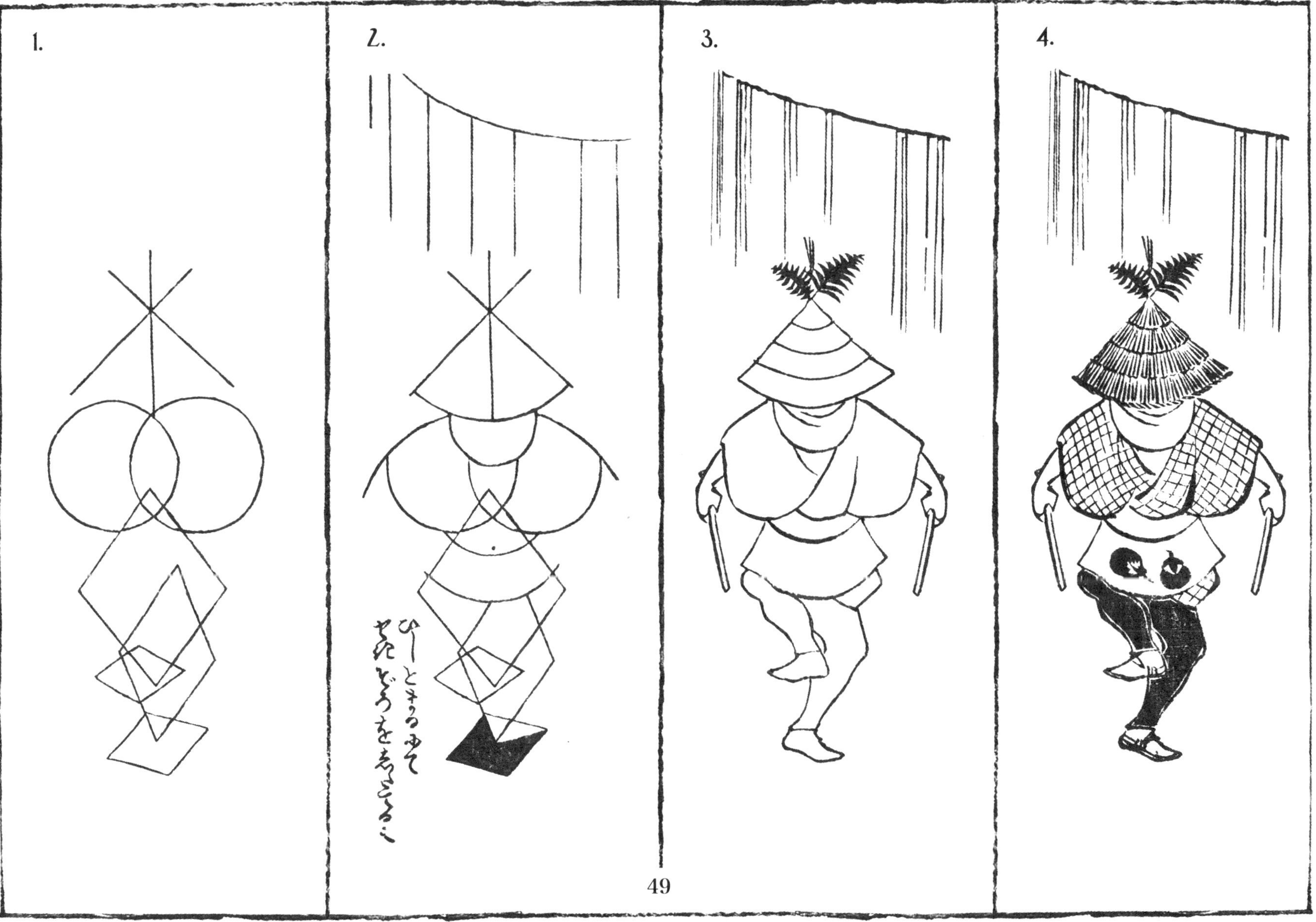

1.
2.
3.
4.
ひーとキつ中て
やれ どろをあつとる

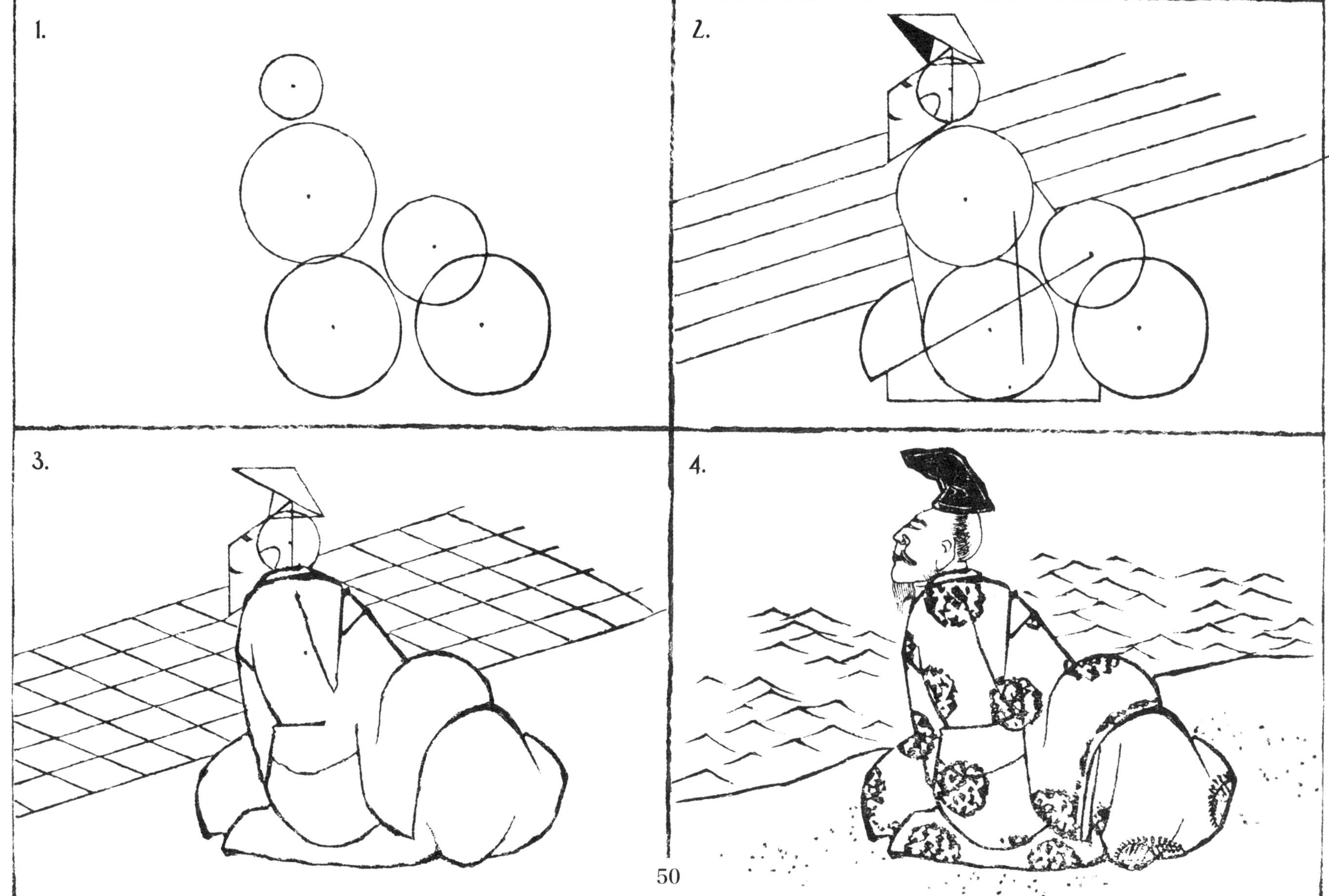

1.
2.
3.
4.
50

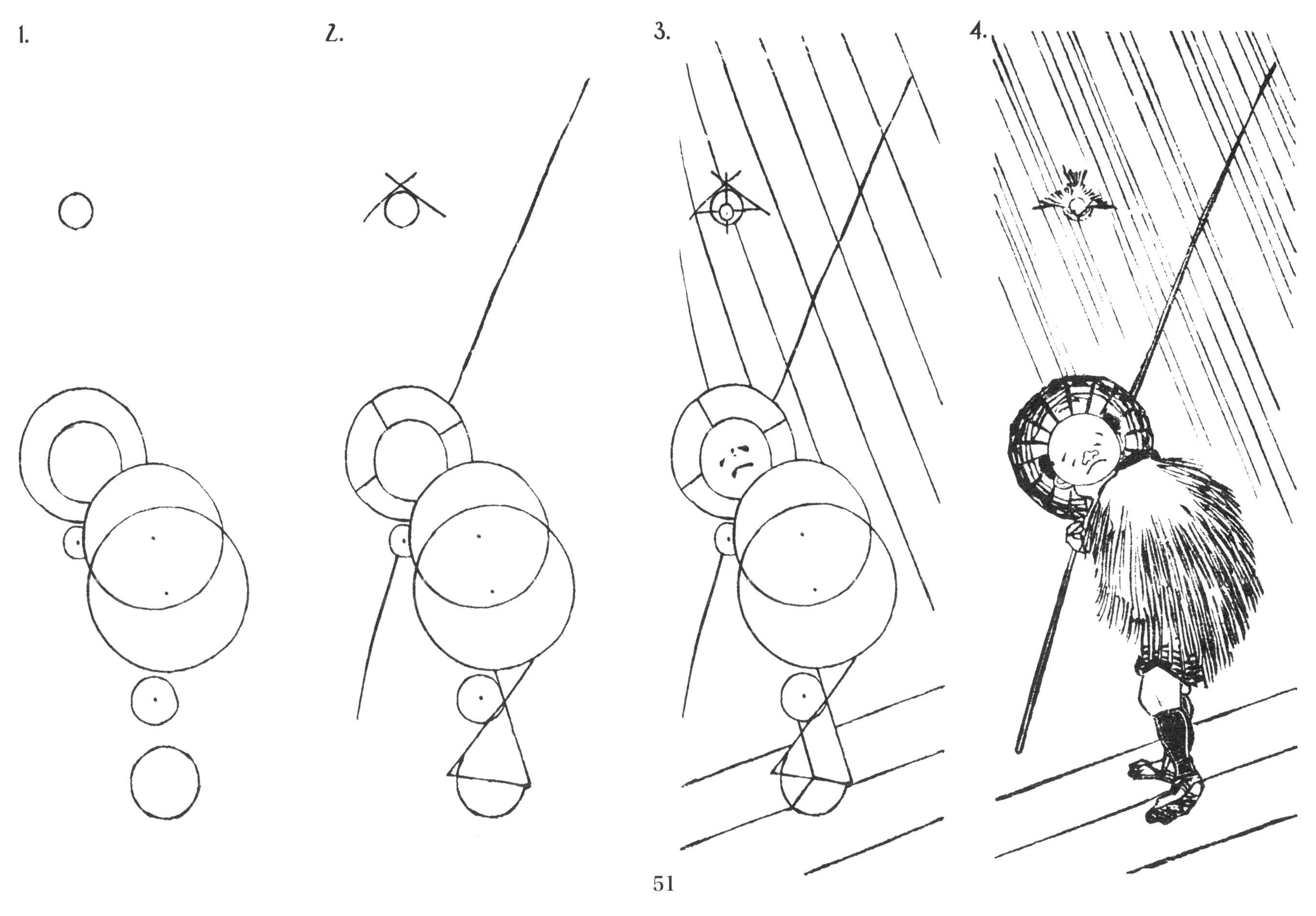

1.
2.
3.
4.

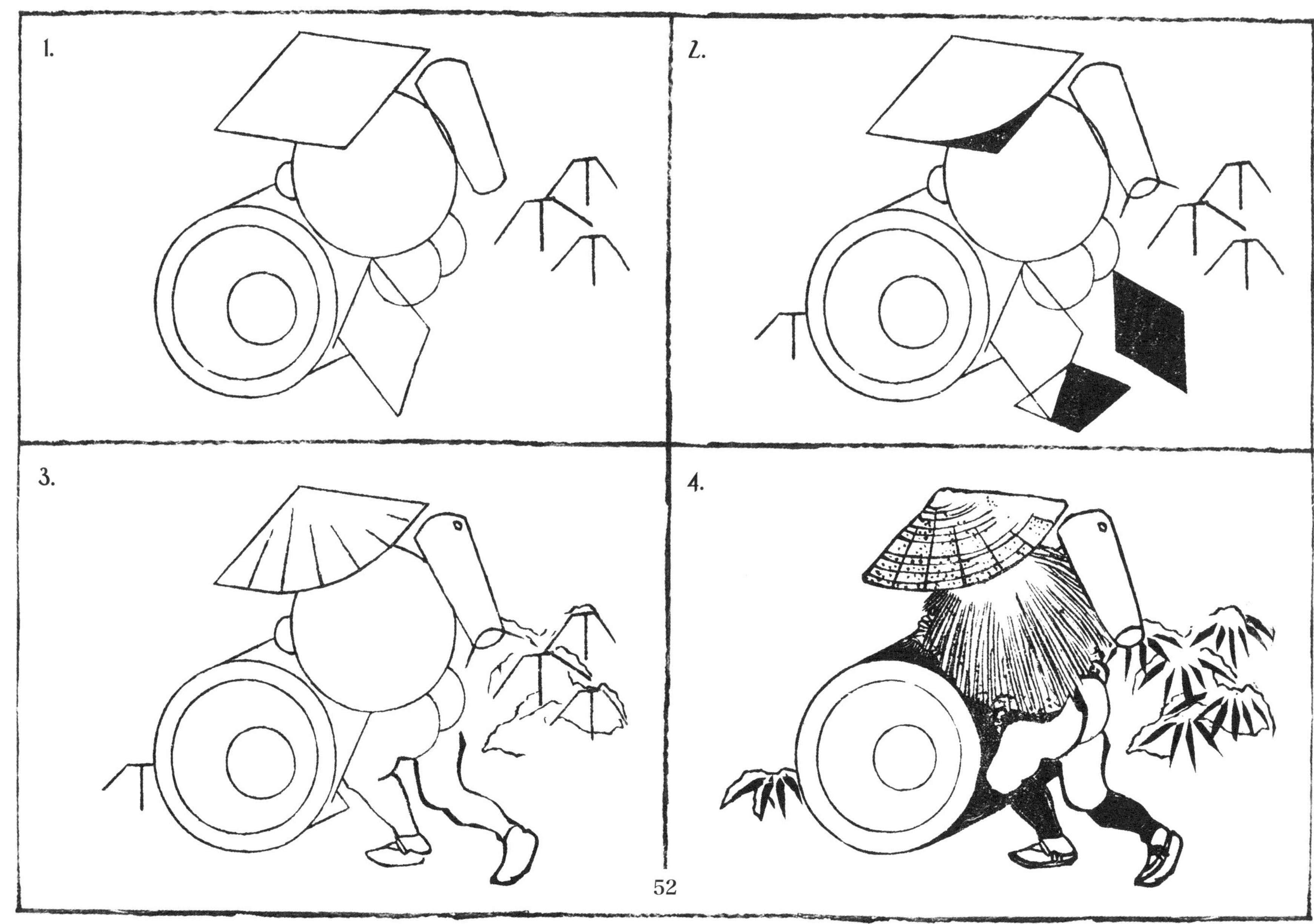

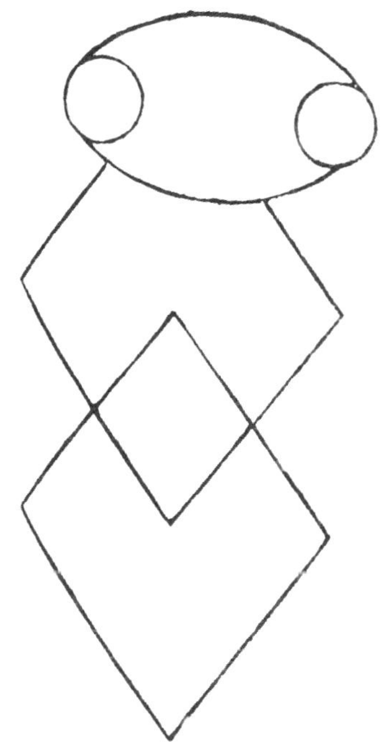

1.

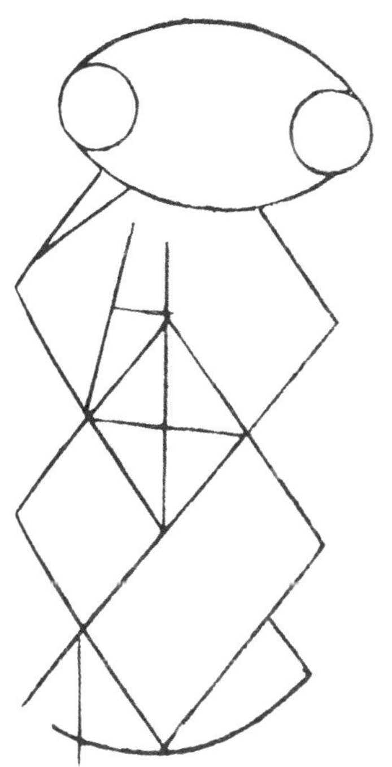

2.

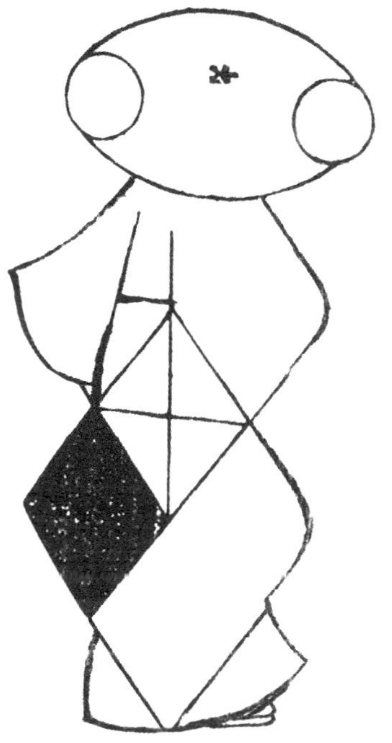

3.

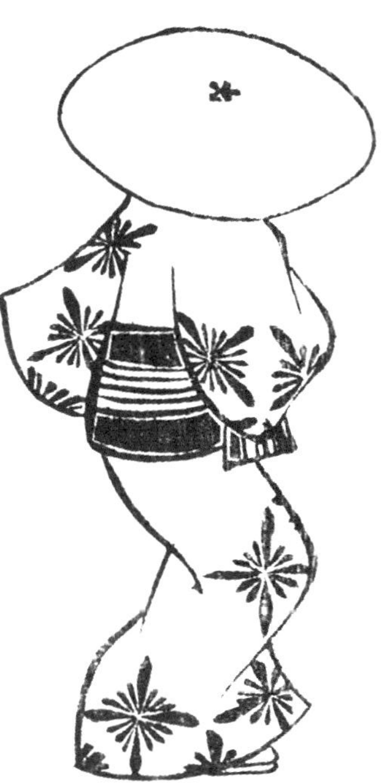

4.

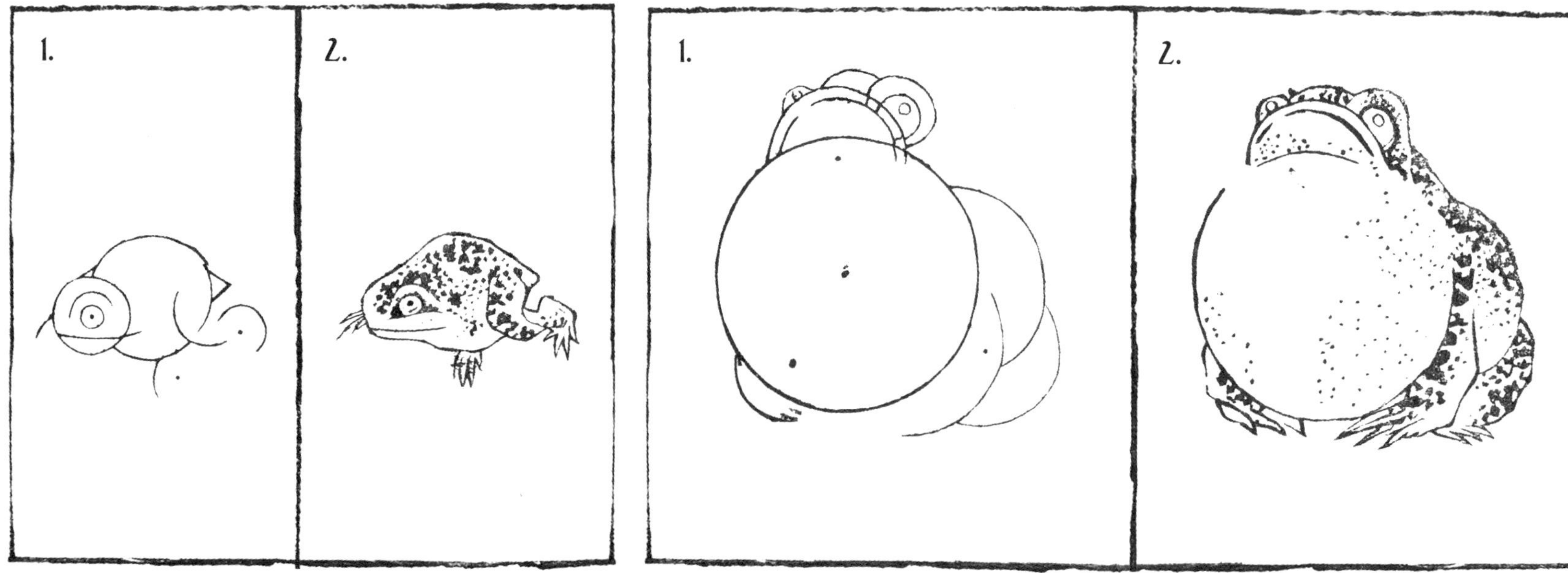

1.
2.
1.
2.

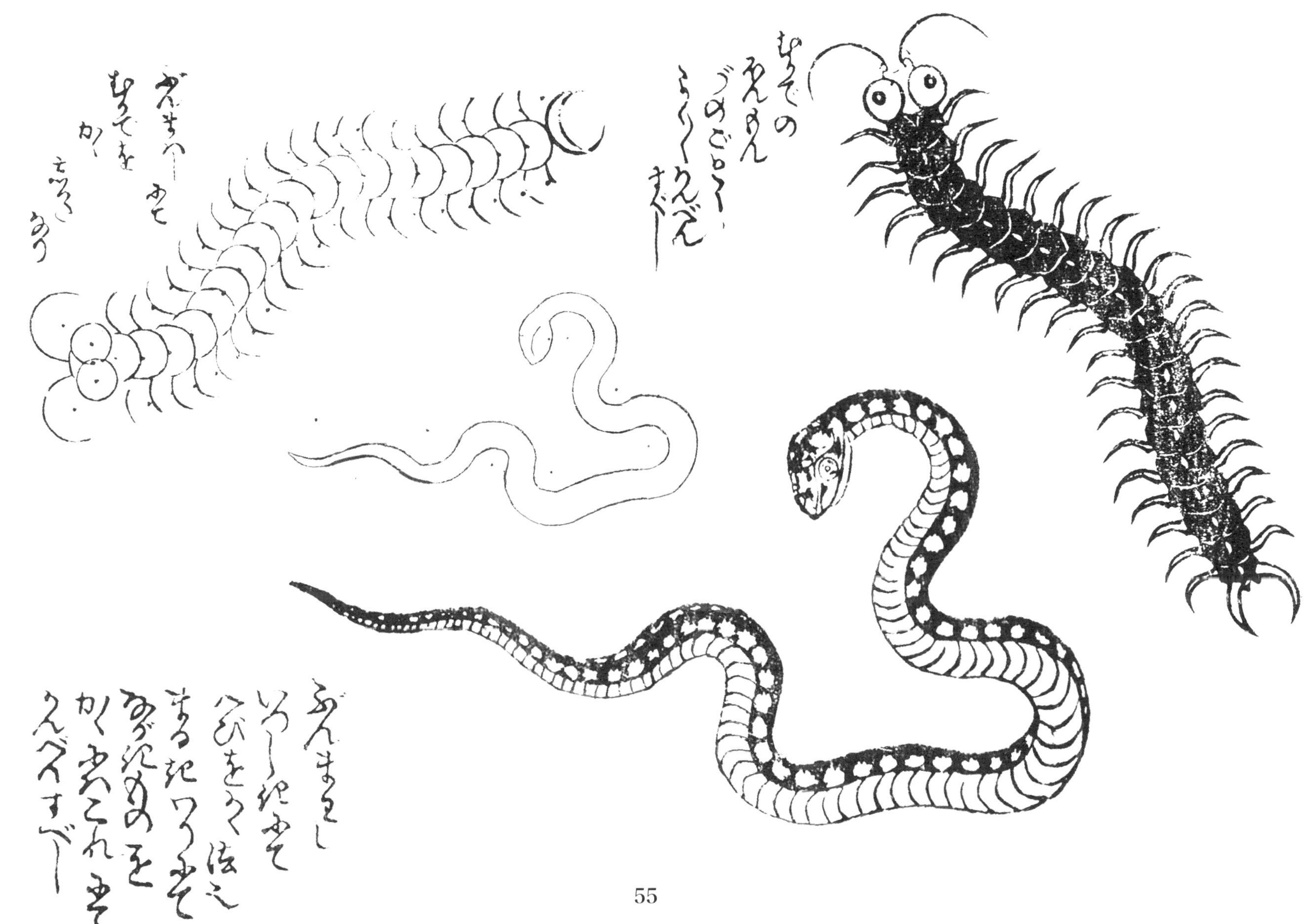

By using shapes and curves, all manner of
different poses and positions can be created.
Notice here how the varying sizes of the circles
also help to denote perspective, with the larger
circles ultimately forming the body parts that
appear closer to the viewer.

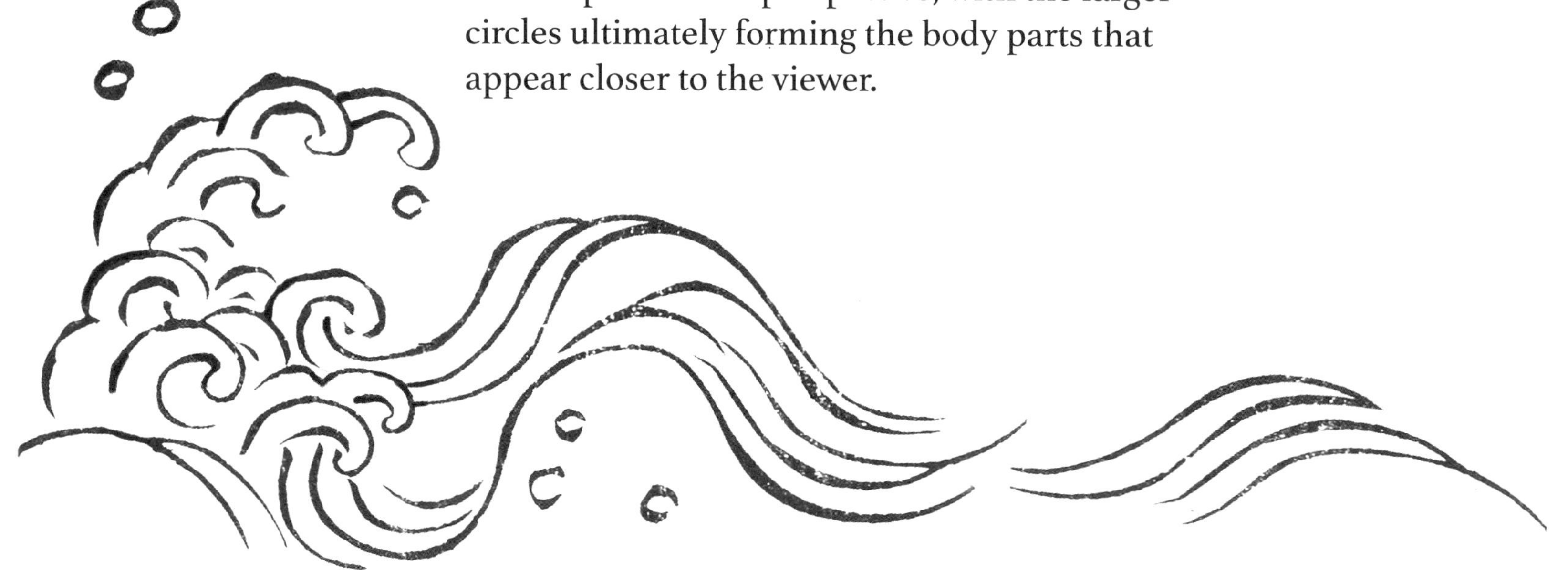

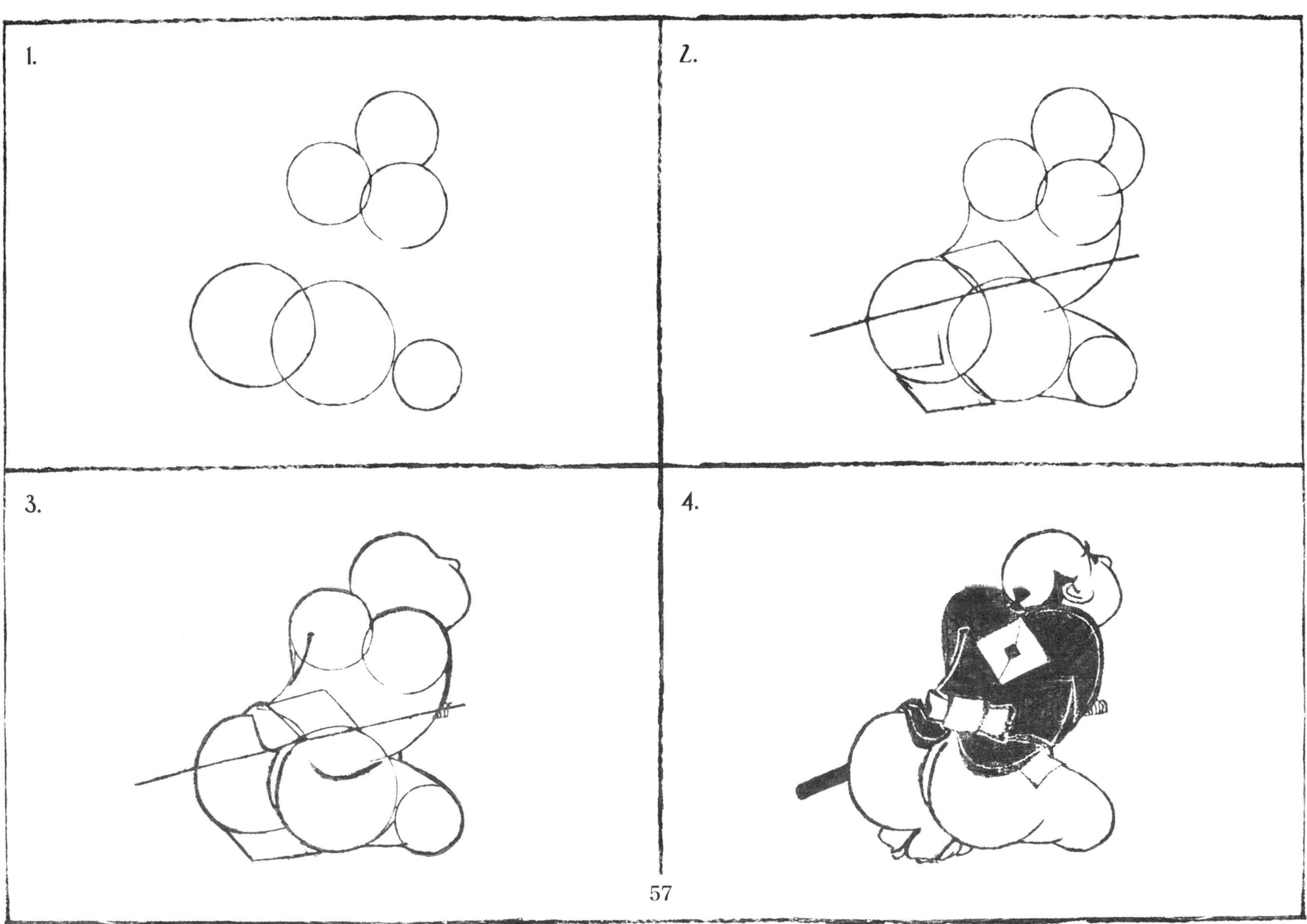

1.
2.
3.
4.

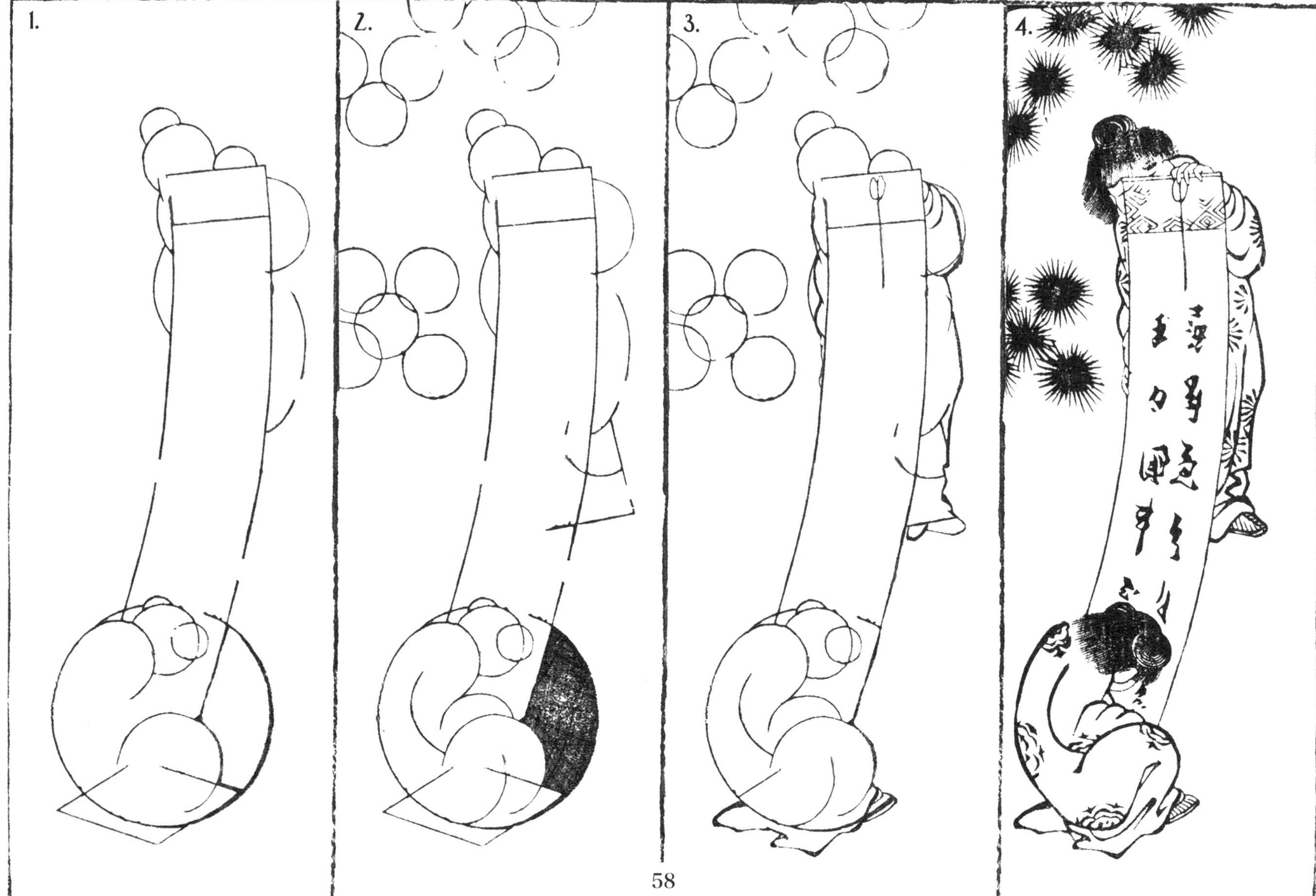

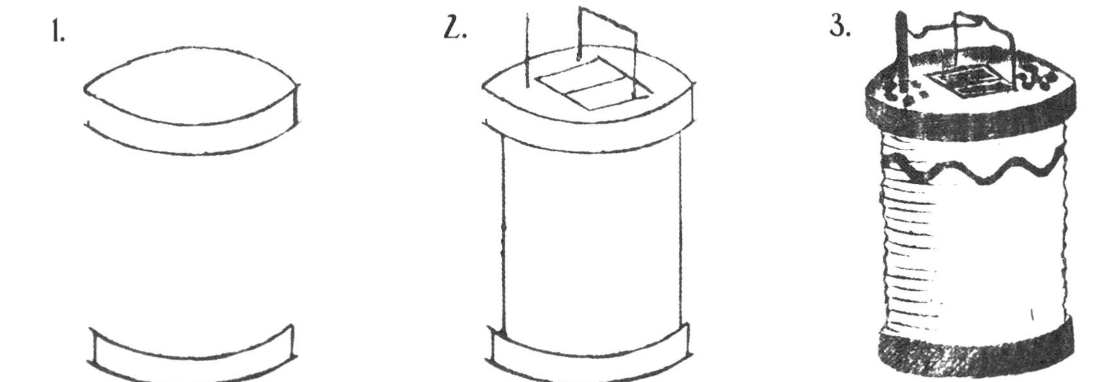

1.
2.
3.

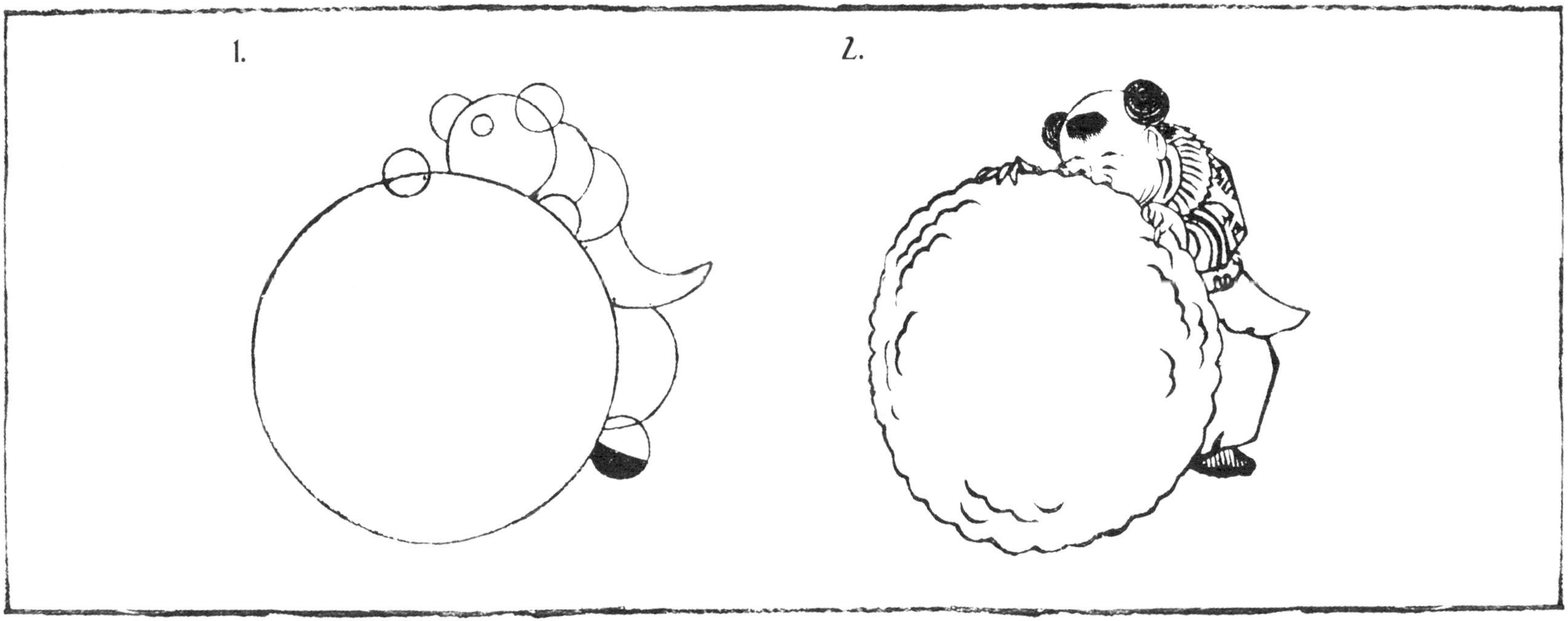

1.
2.

1.

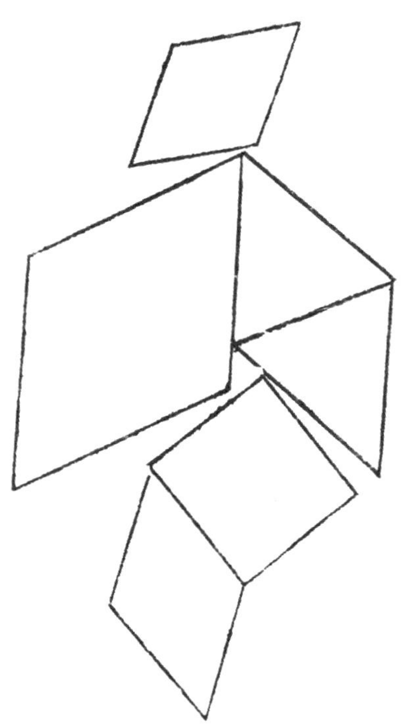

2.

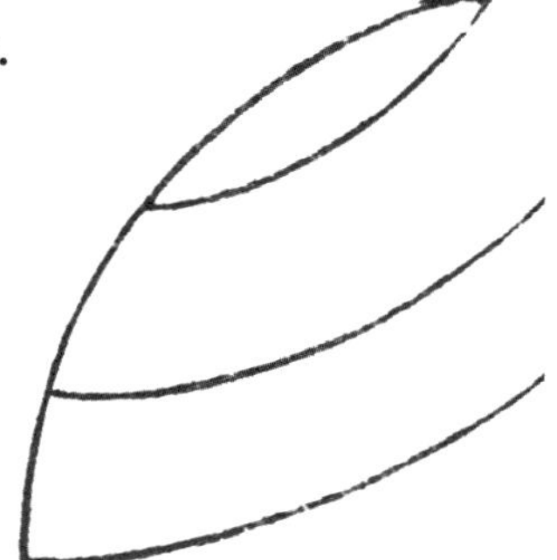

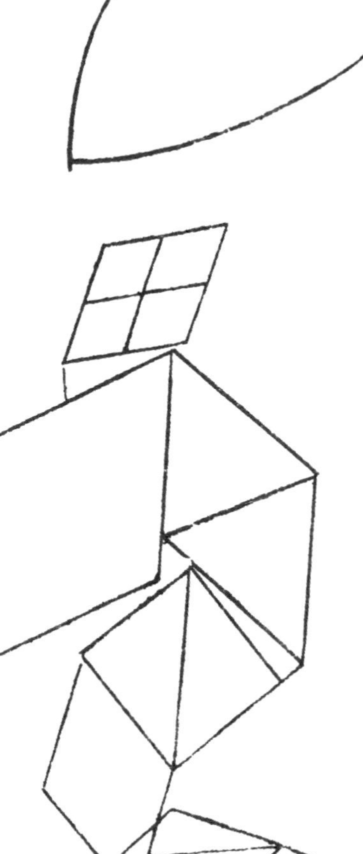

3.

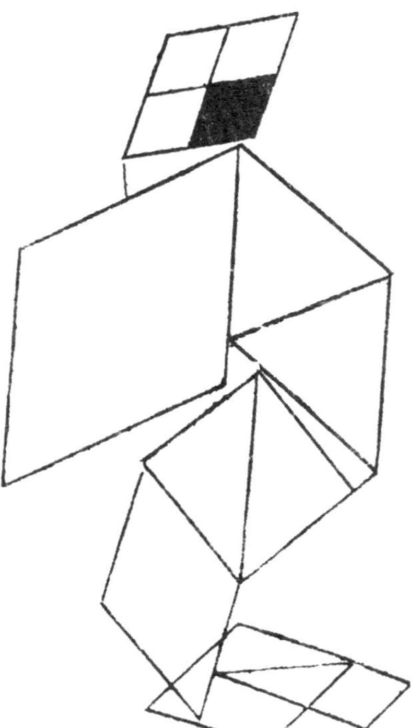

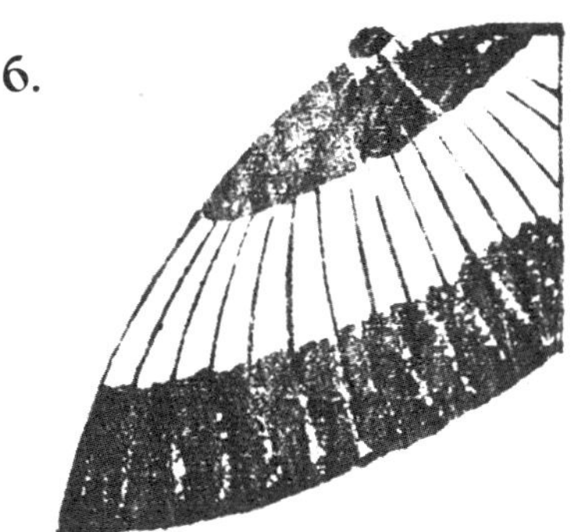

4.

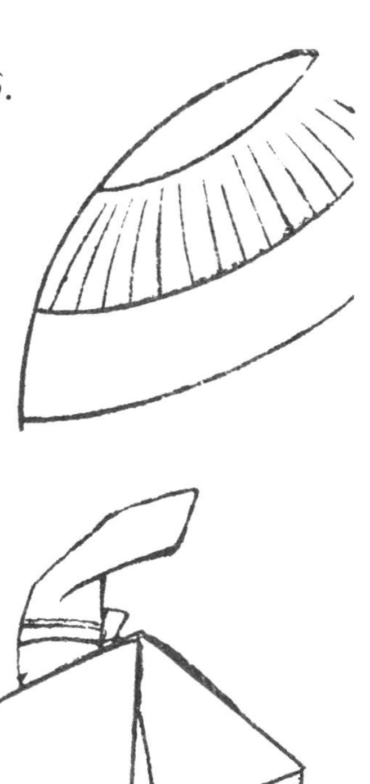

5.

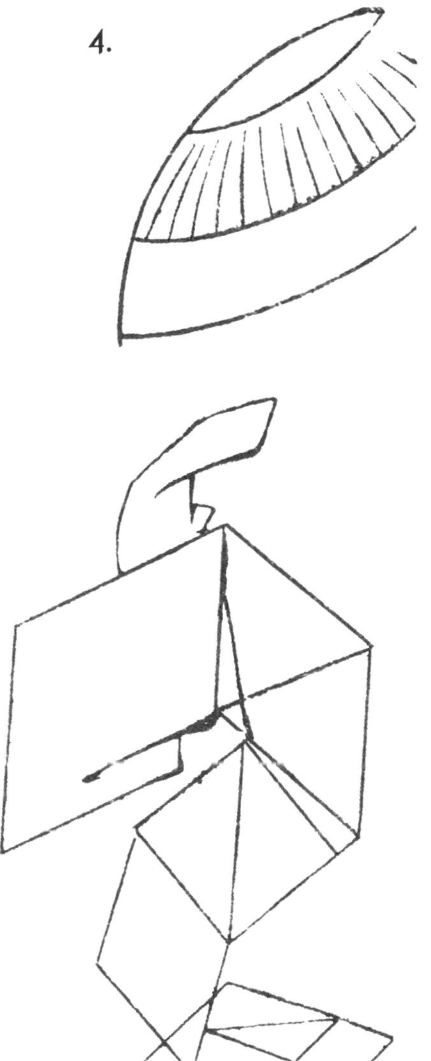

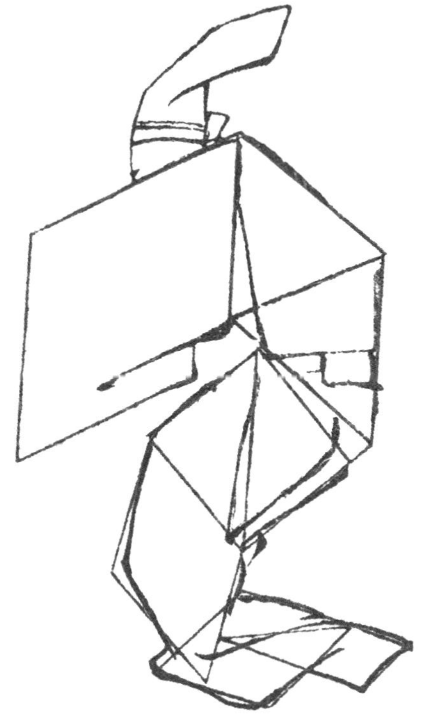

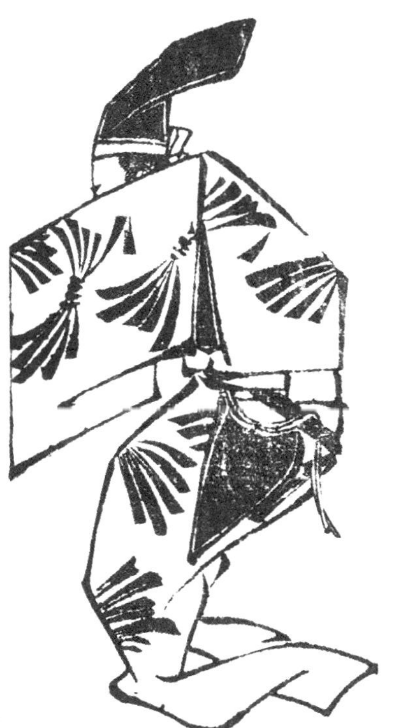

6.

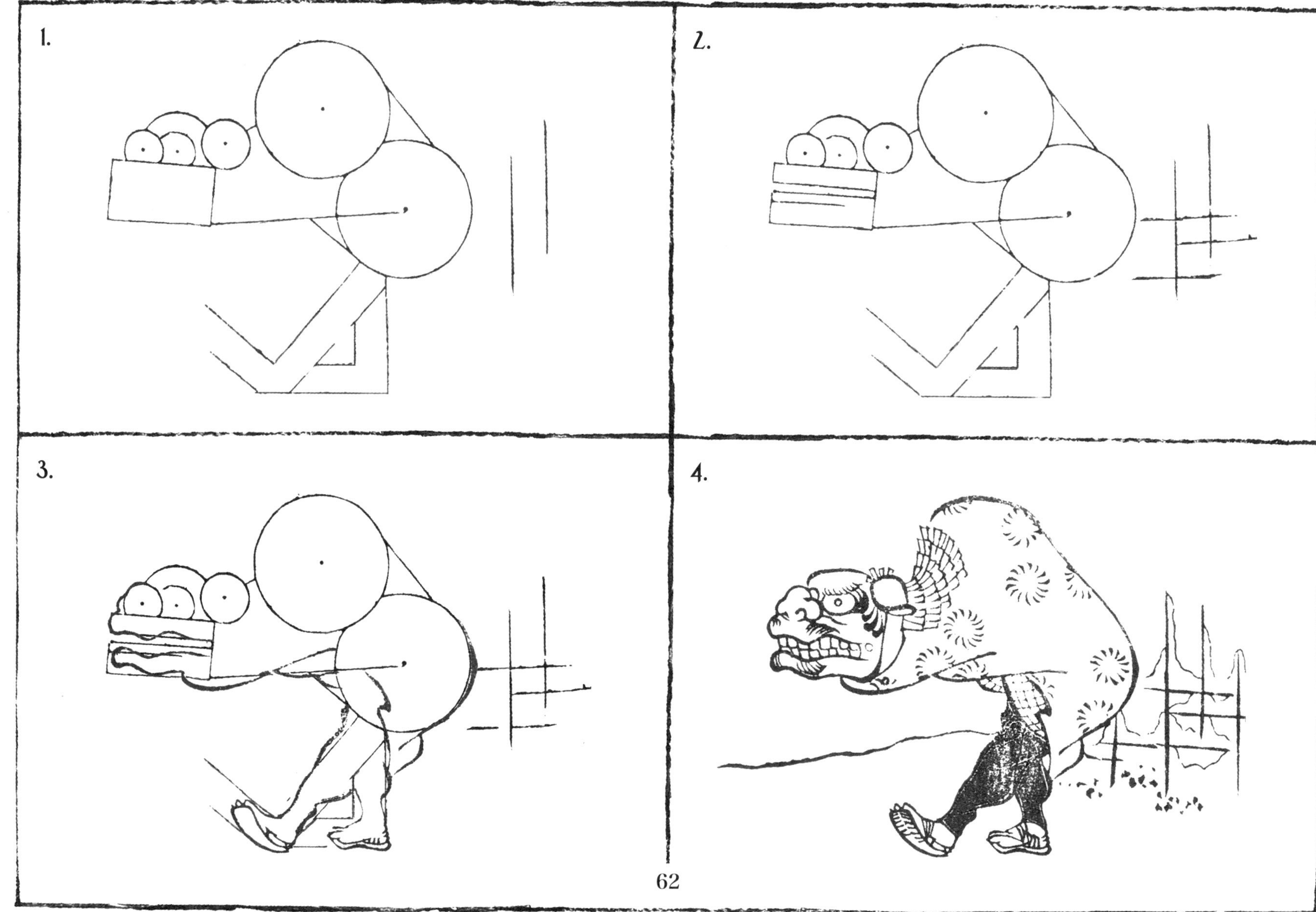

1.
2.
3.
4.

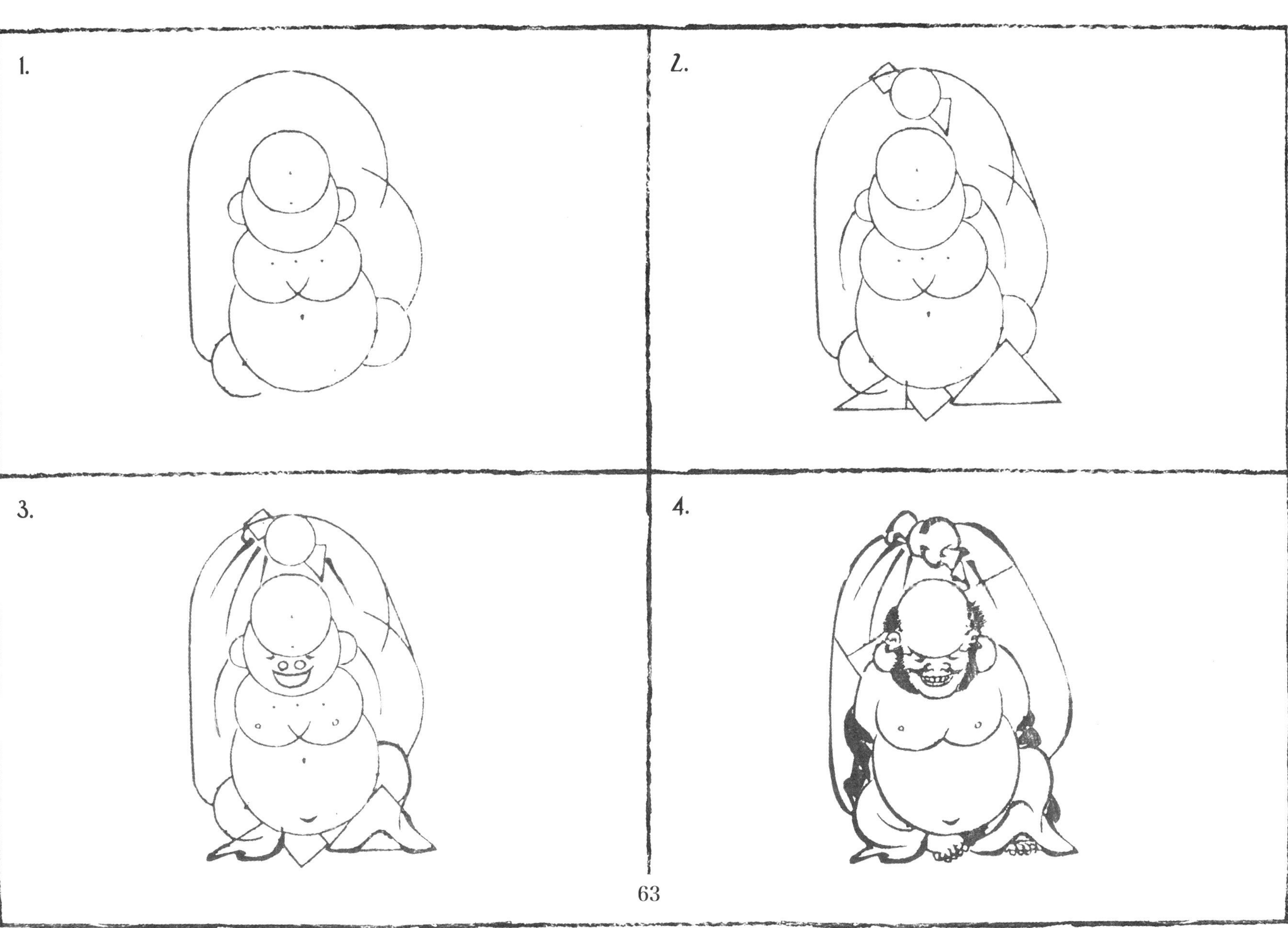

1.
2.
3.
4.

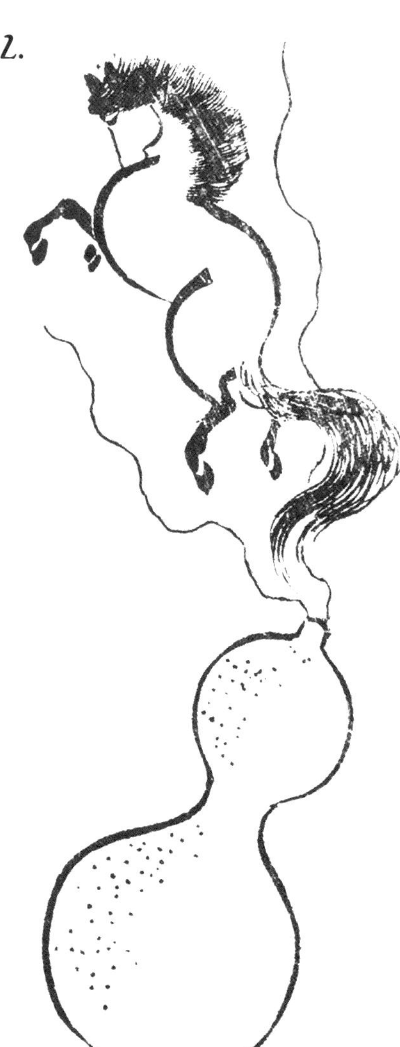

1.

2.

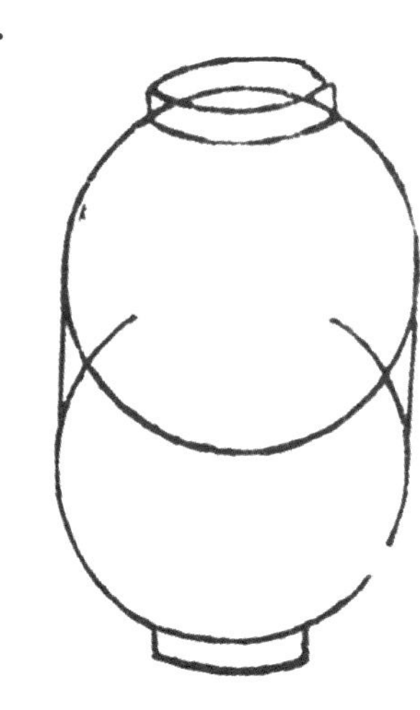

1.

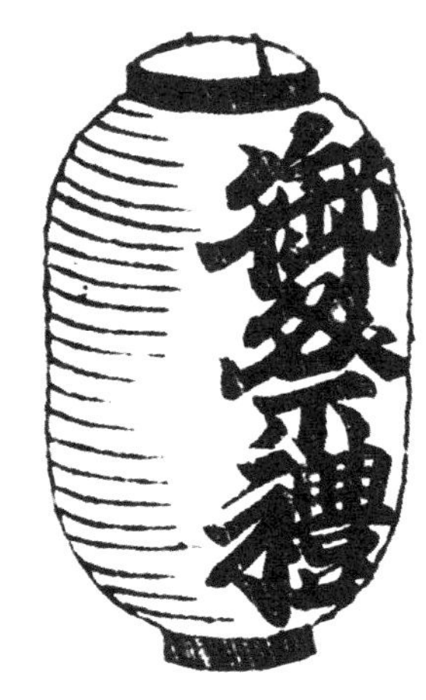

2.

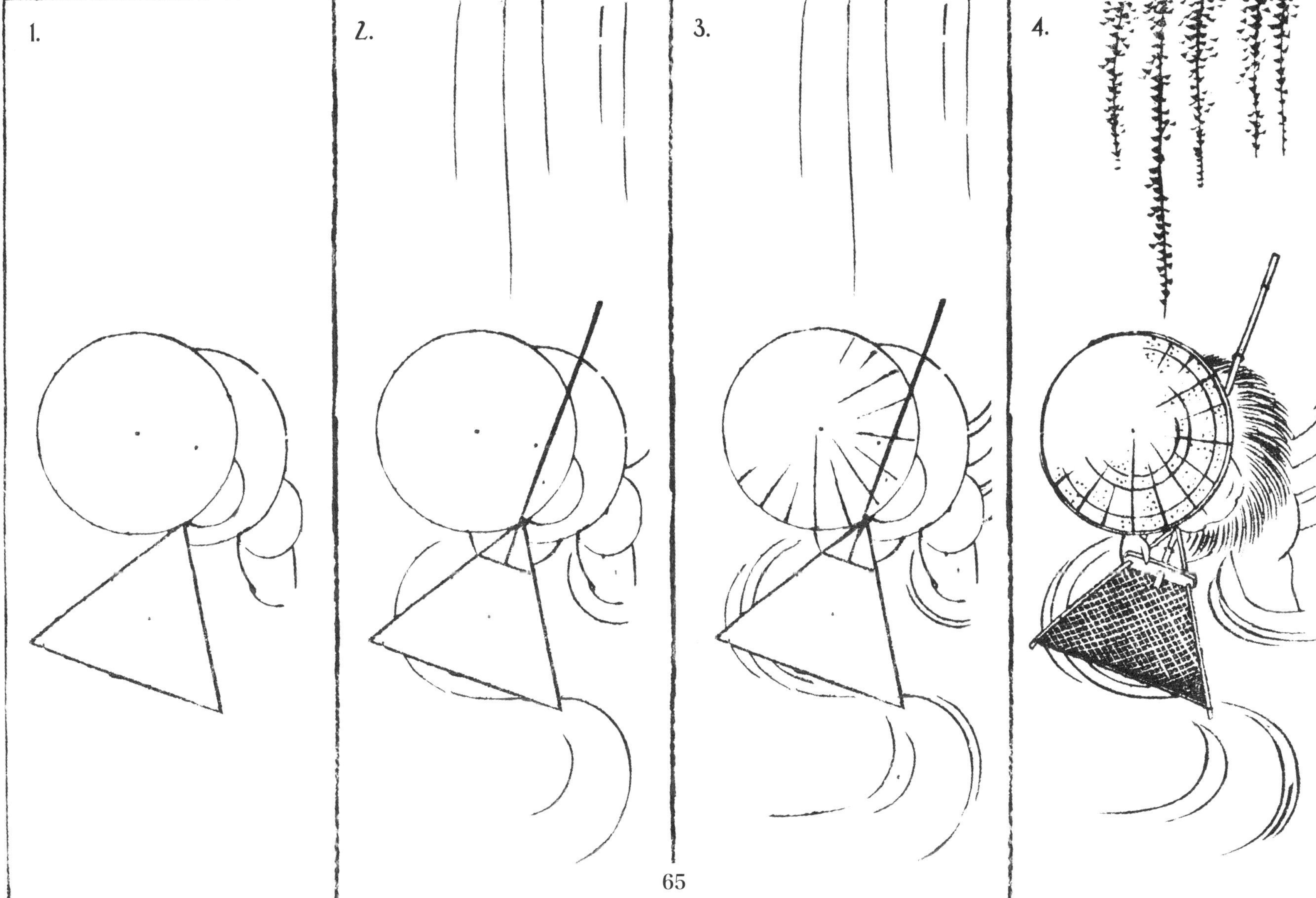

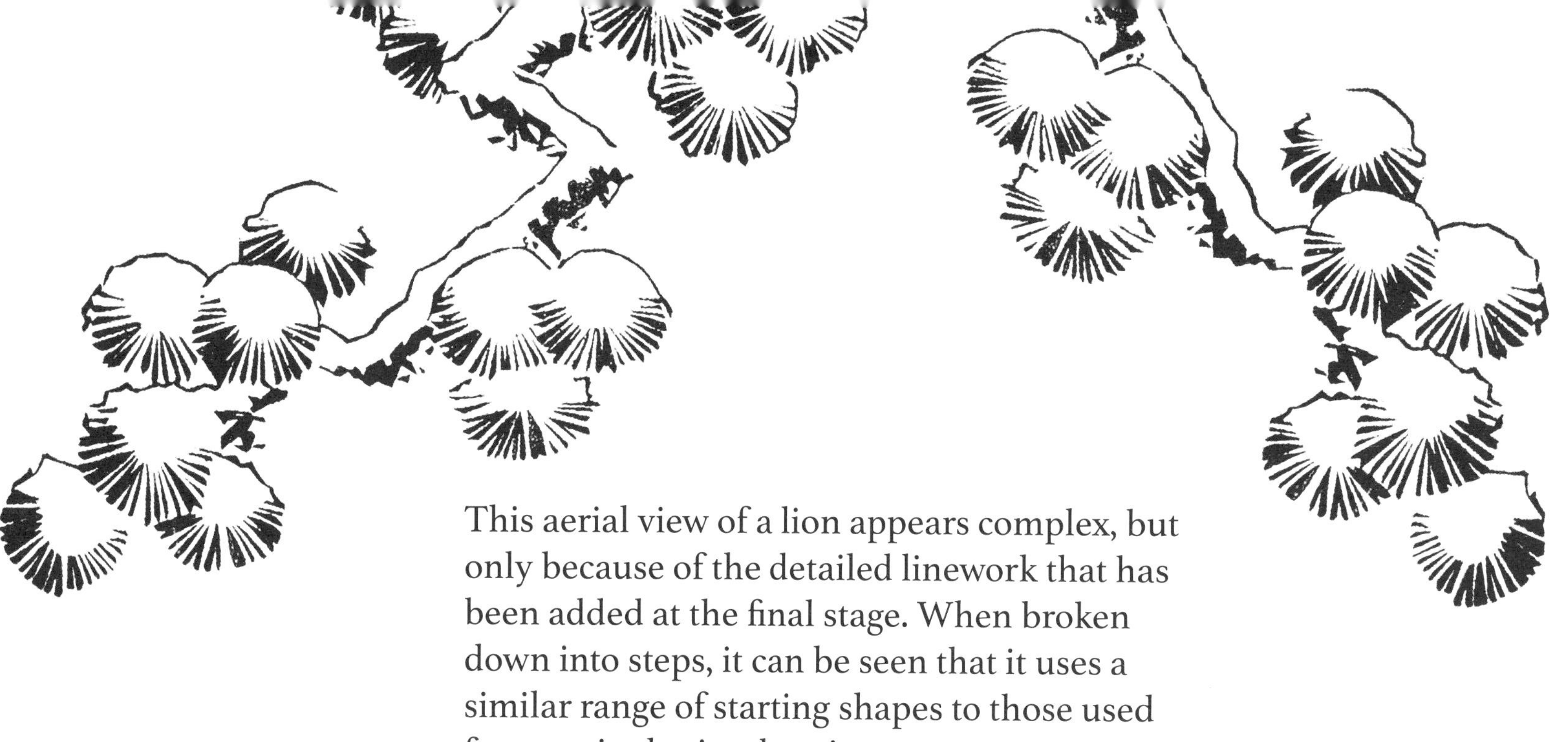

This aerial view of a lion appears complex, but only because of the detailed linework that has been added at the final stage. When broken down into steps, it can be seen that it uses a similar range of starting shapes to those used for seemingly simpler pieces.

1.

2.

3.

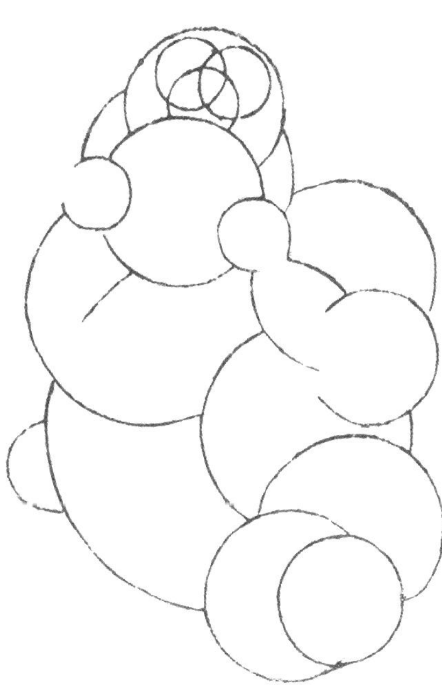
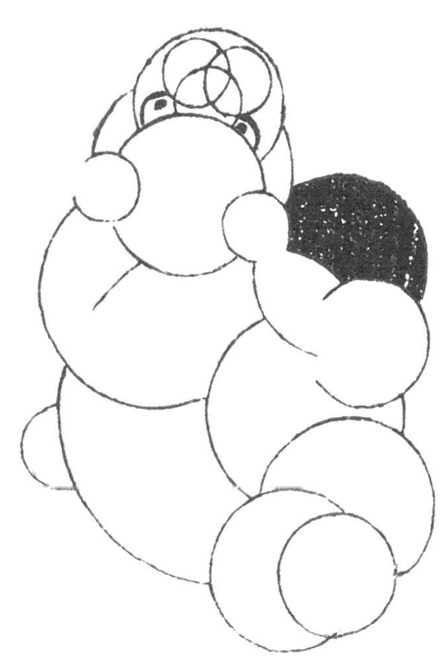
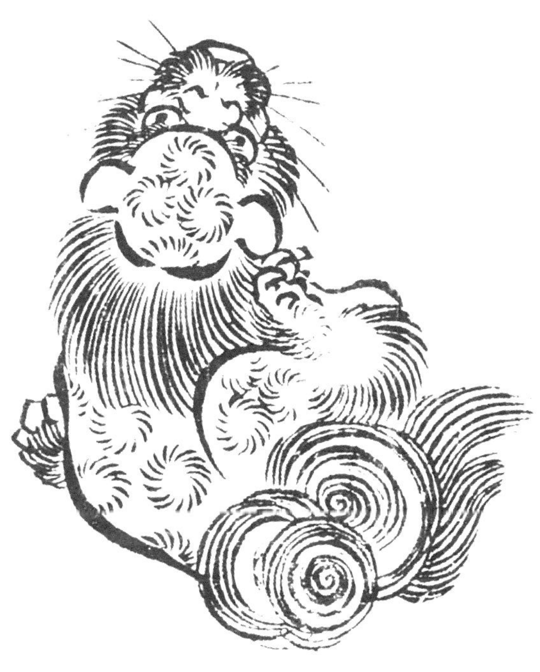

1.

2.

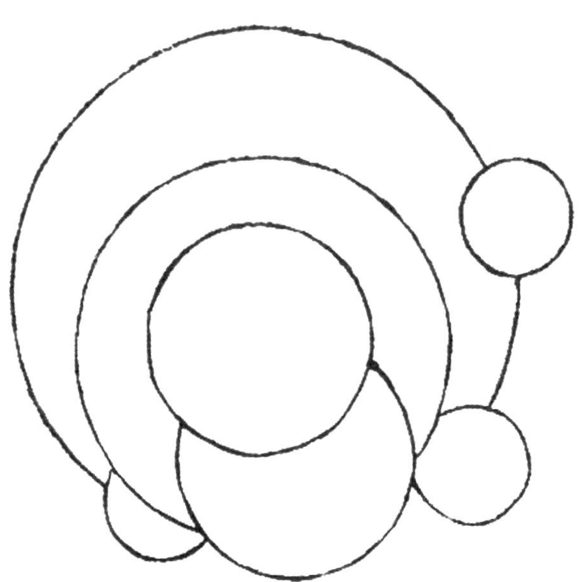

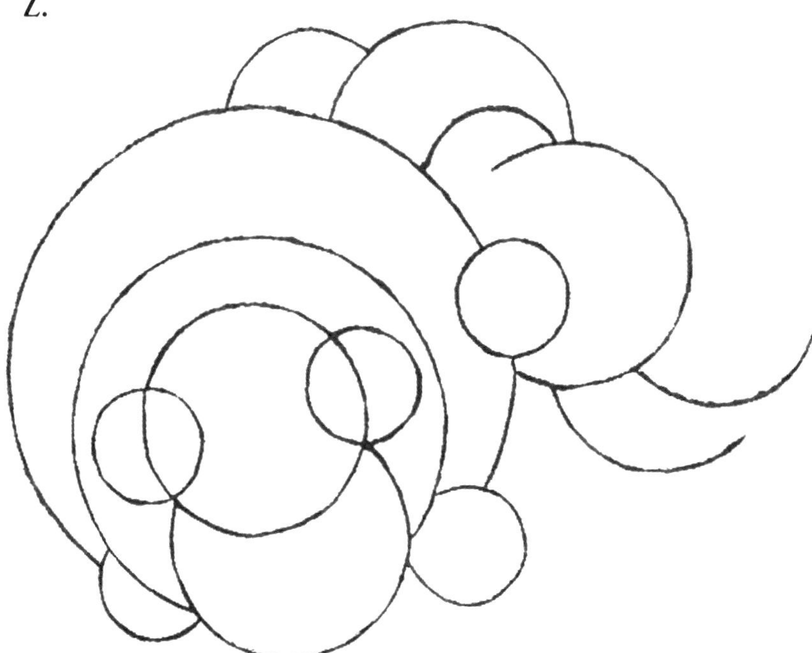

3.

4.

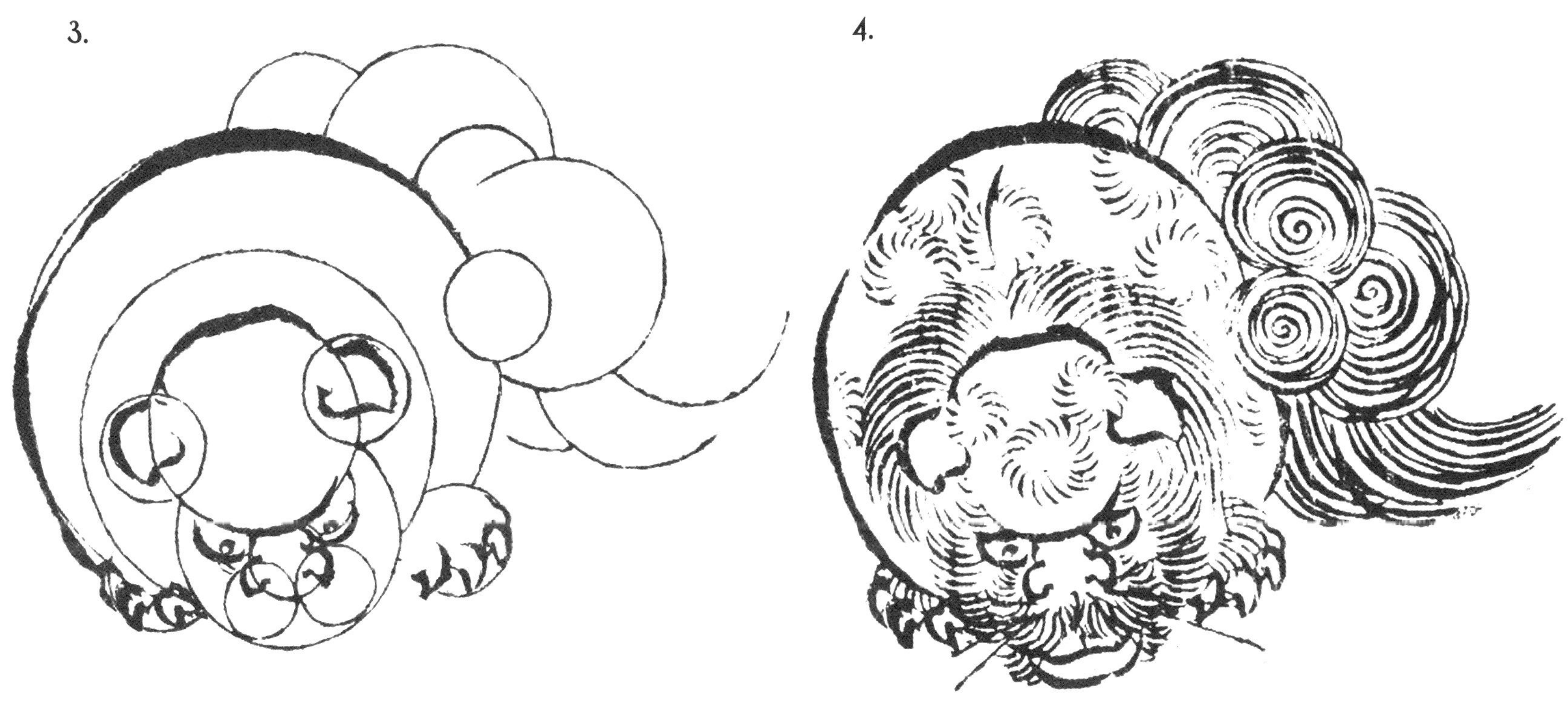

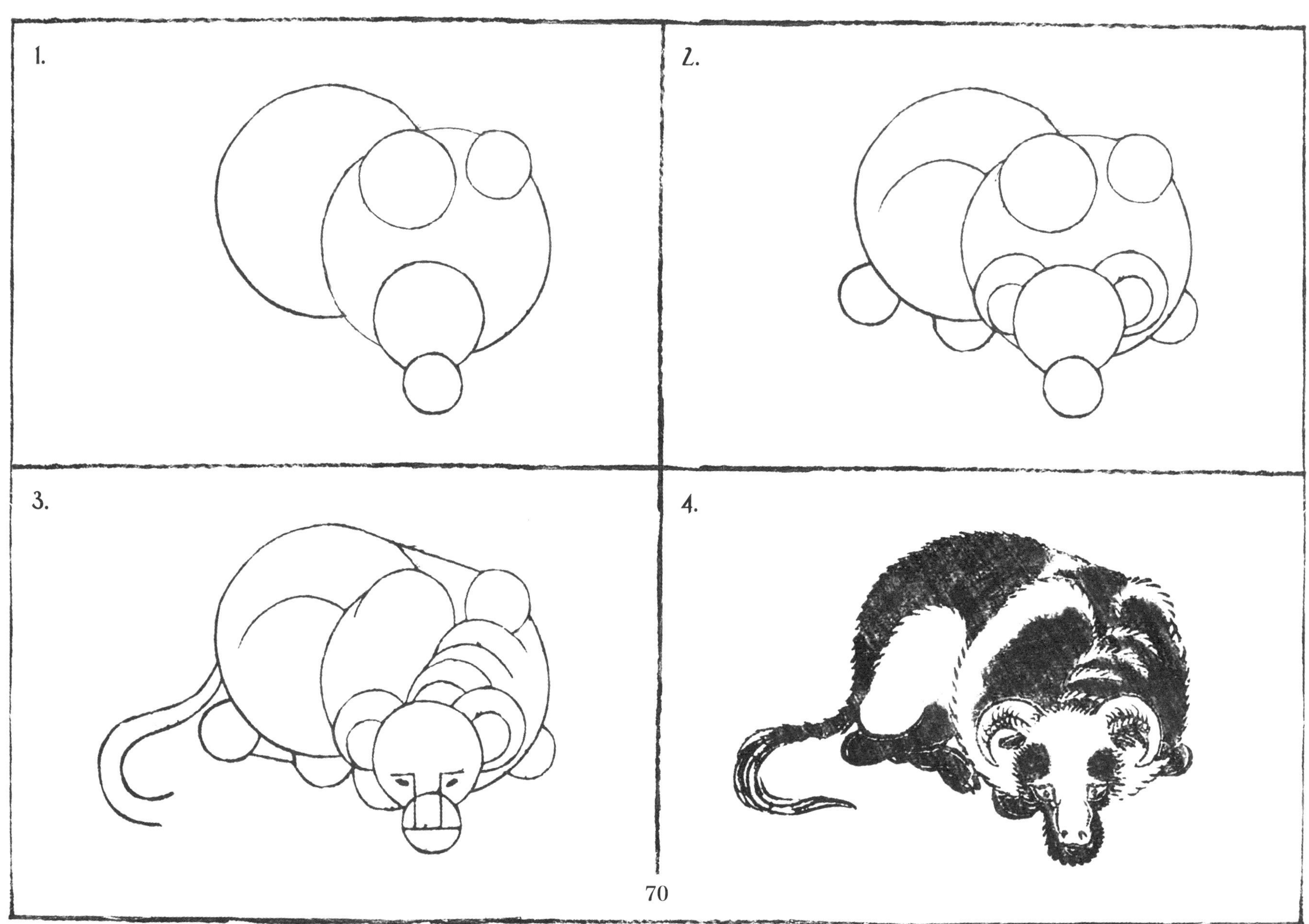

1.
2.
3.
4.

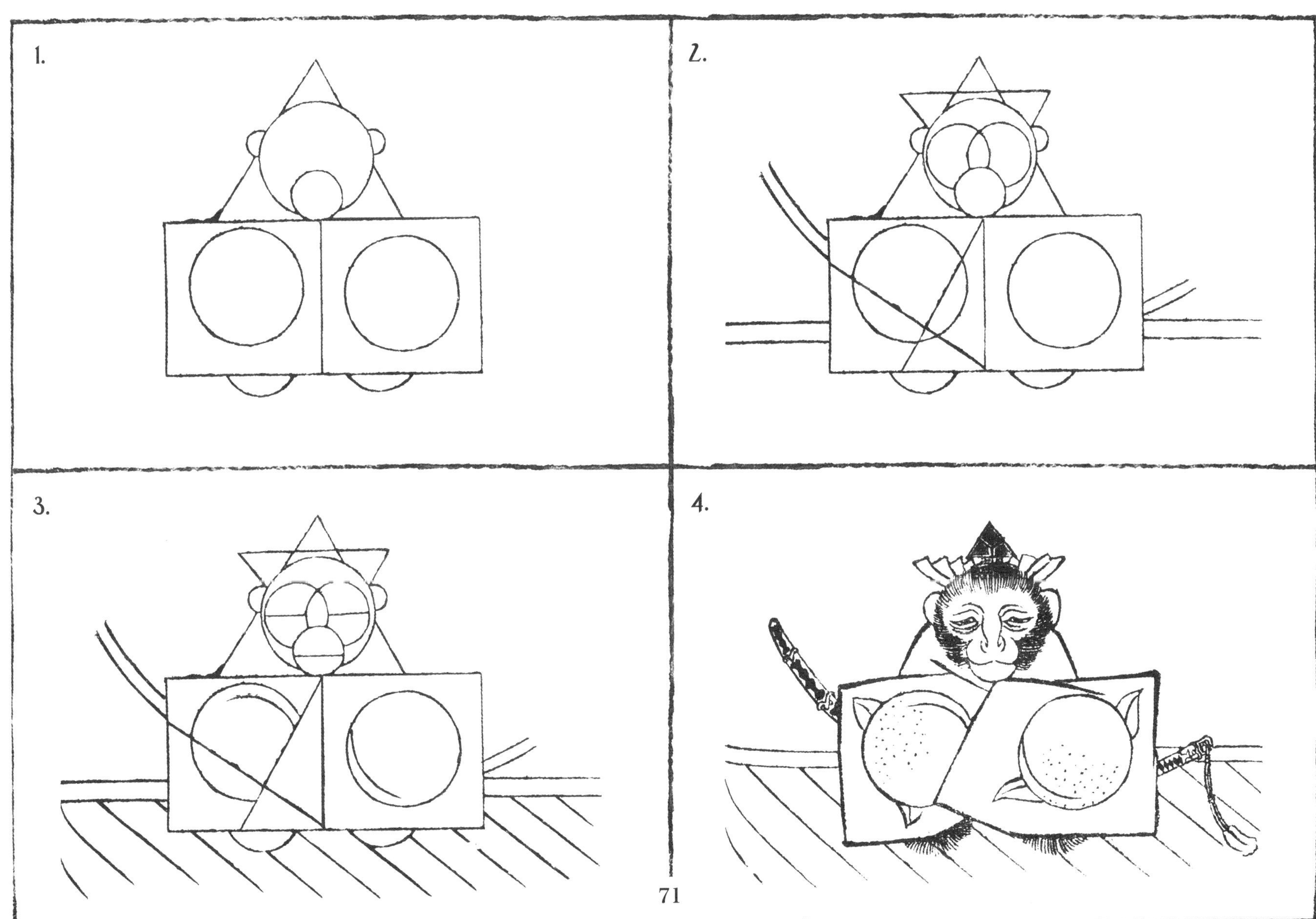

1.
2.
3.
4.

1.

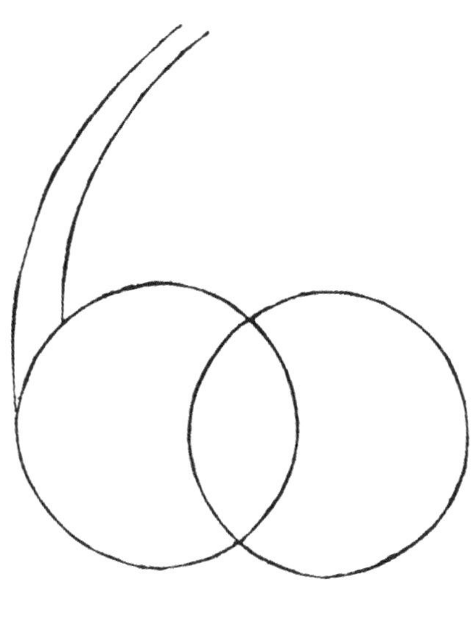

2.

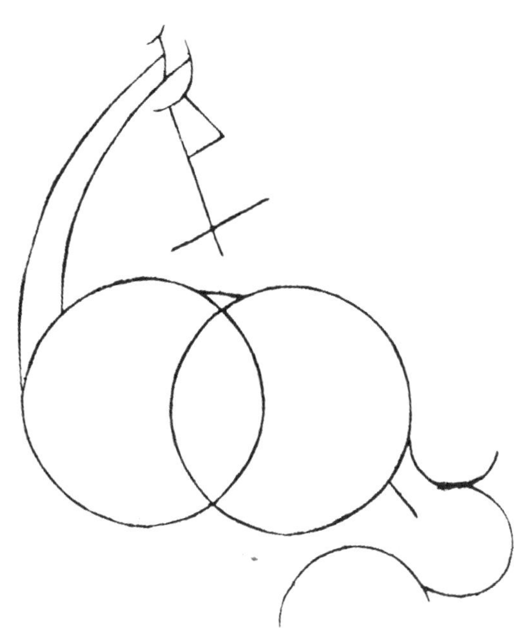

3.

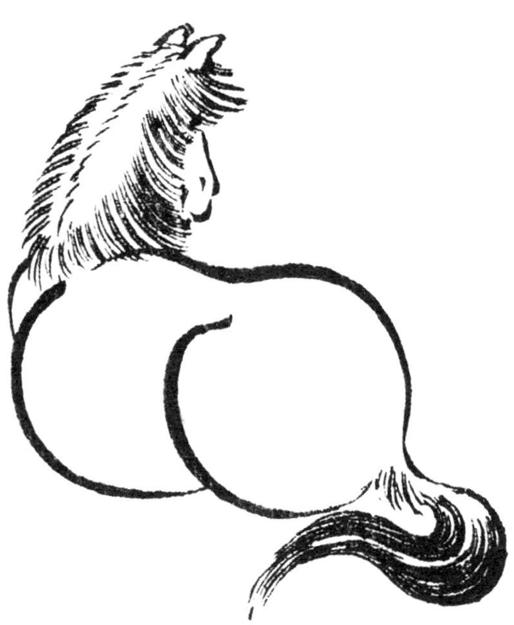

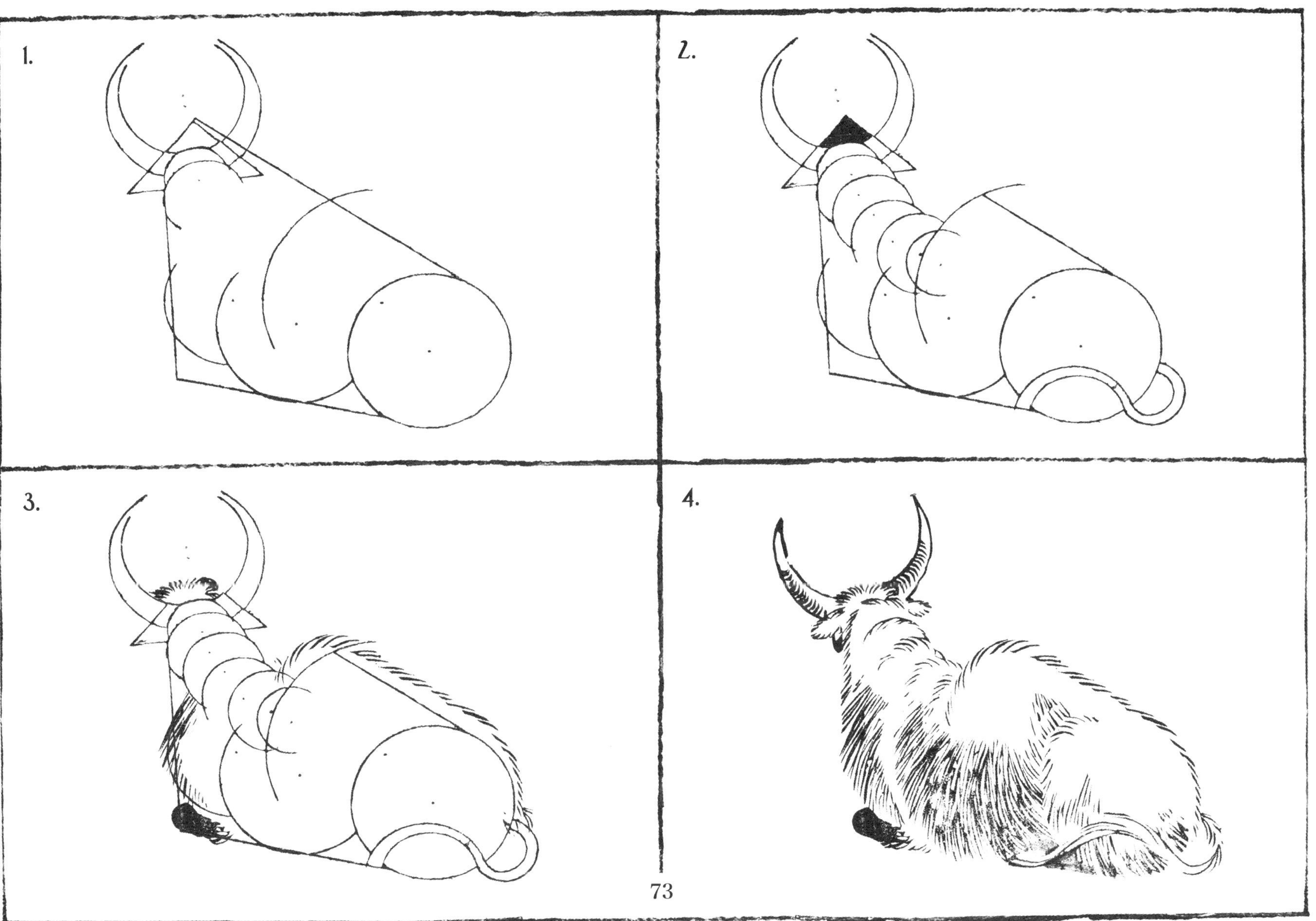

1.
2.
3.
4.

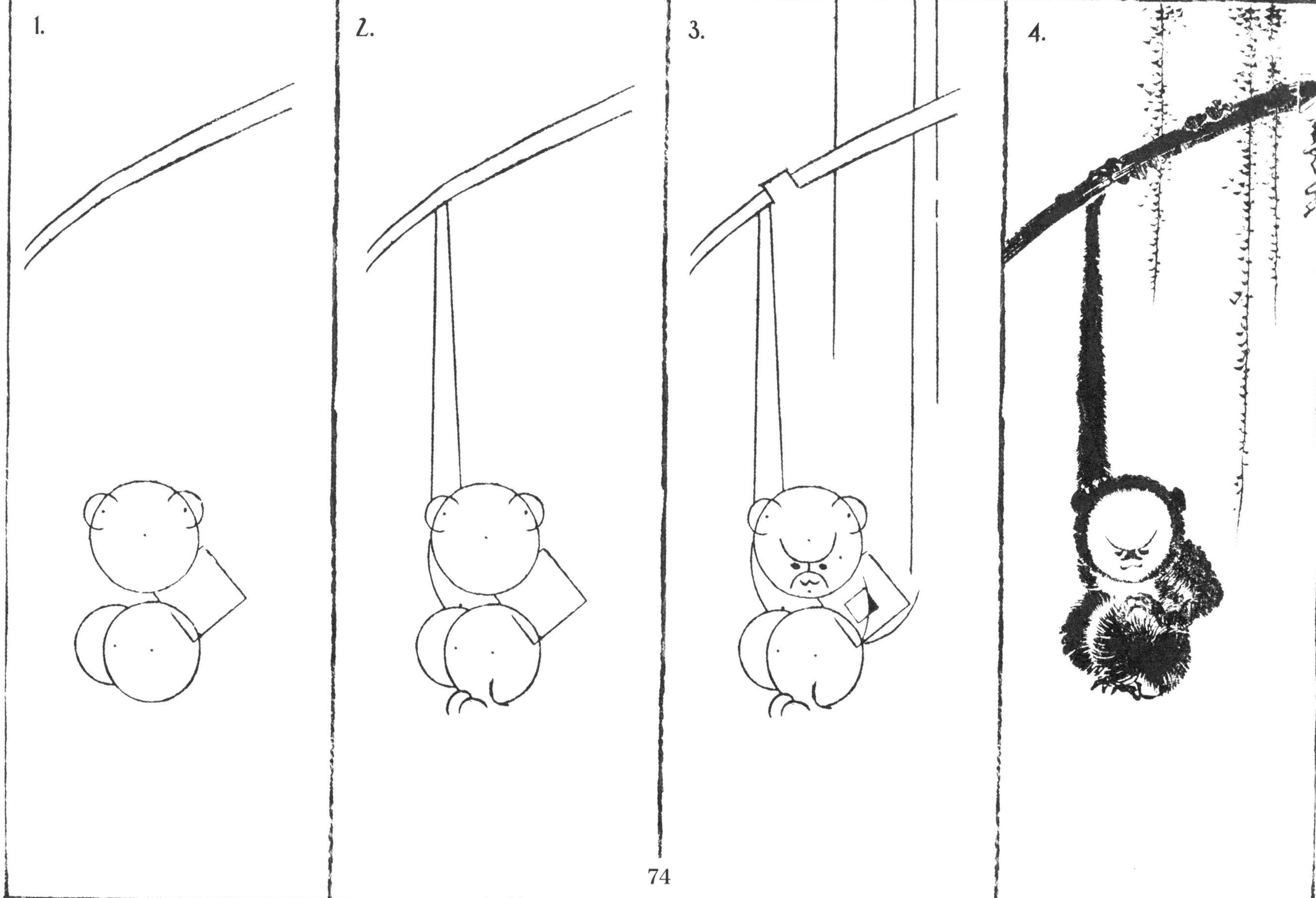

1.
2.
3.
4.

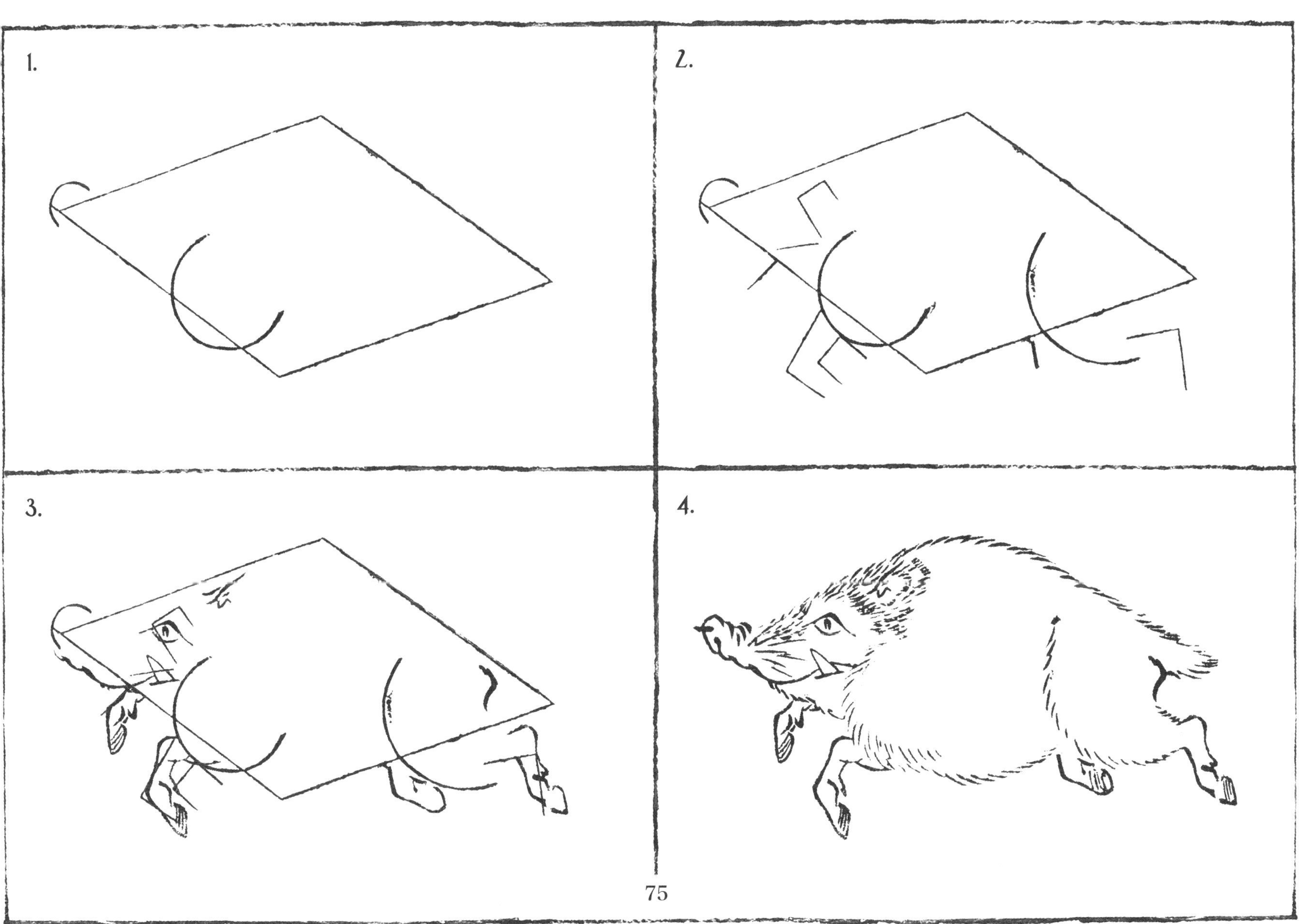

1.
2.
3.
4.

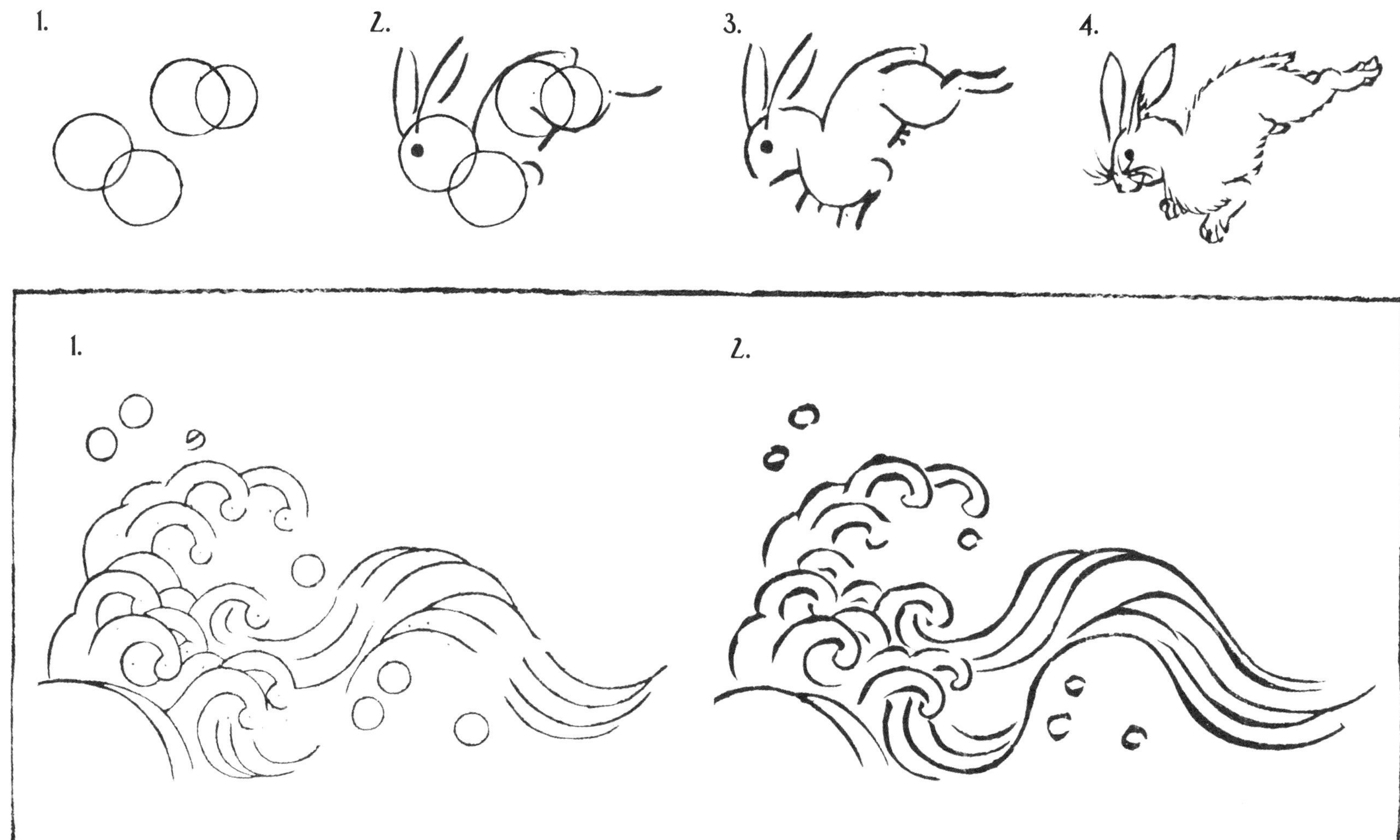

1.
2.
3.
4.
1.
2.

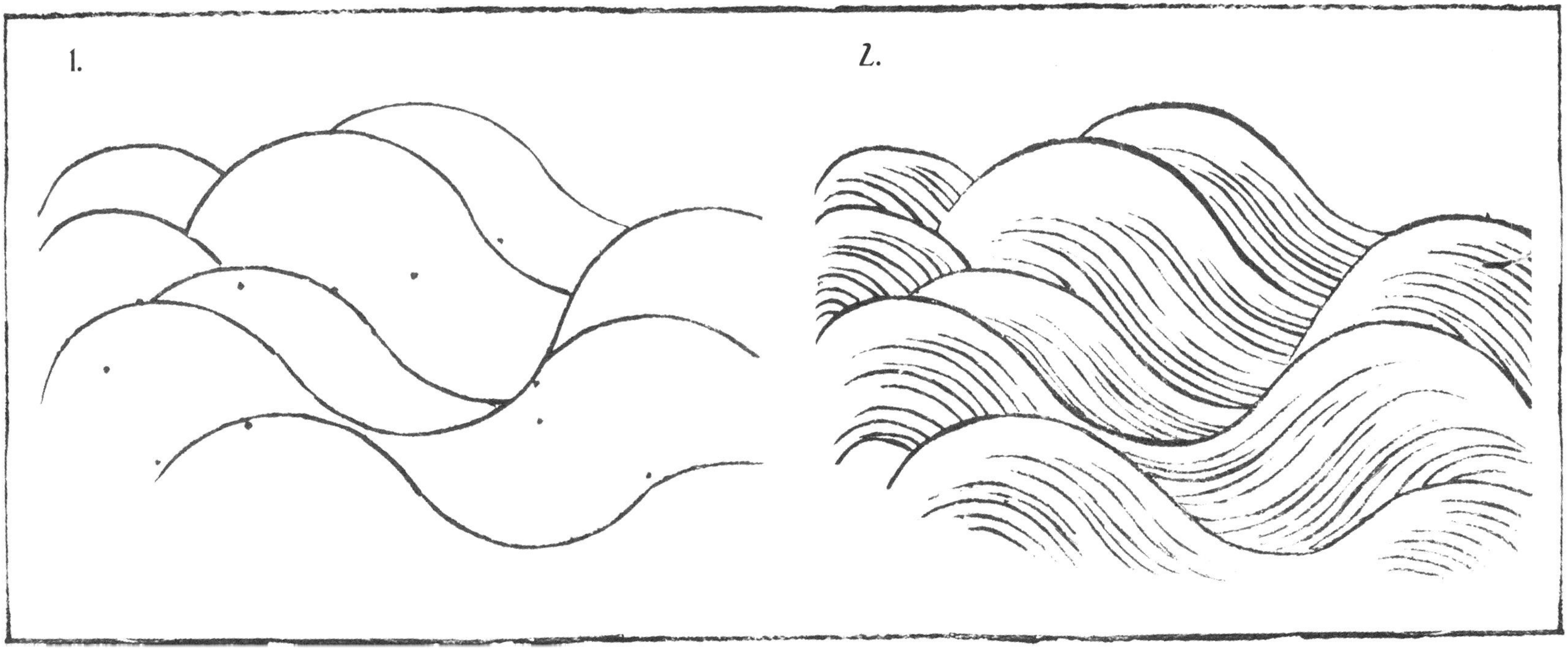

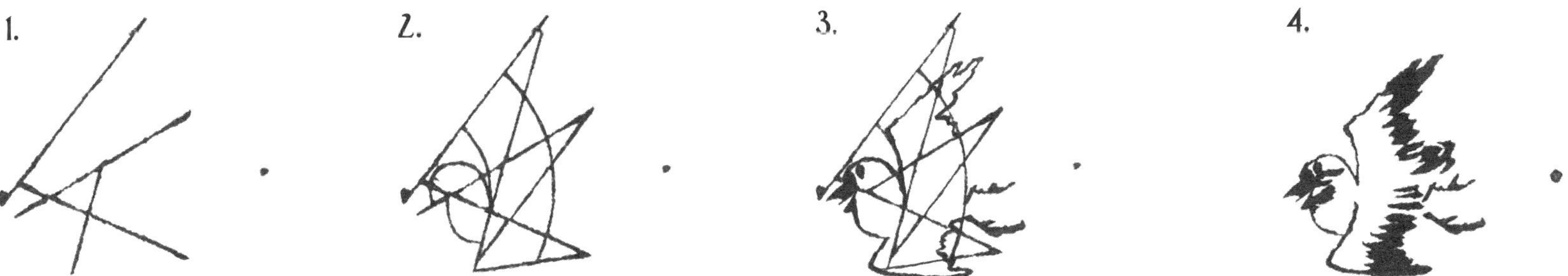

Conclusion

You may not quite be a grand master just yet, but you have discovered that even the very finest art often comes from a starting point of achievable simplicity.

Upon mastering the techniques demonstrated in this book, you should be able to apply them to your own subjects of choice. Consider what else you would like to draw in Hokusai's style, and experiment with which shapes, lines and curves will work best to take you there.

With practice, perseverence and lots of experimentation you too can create the sort of mini masterpieces that Hokusai would be proud of.

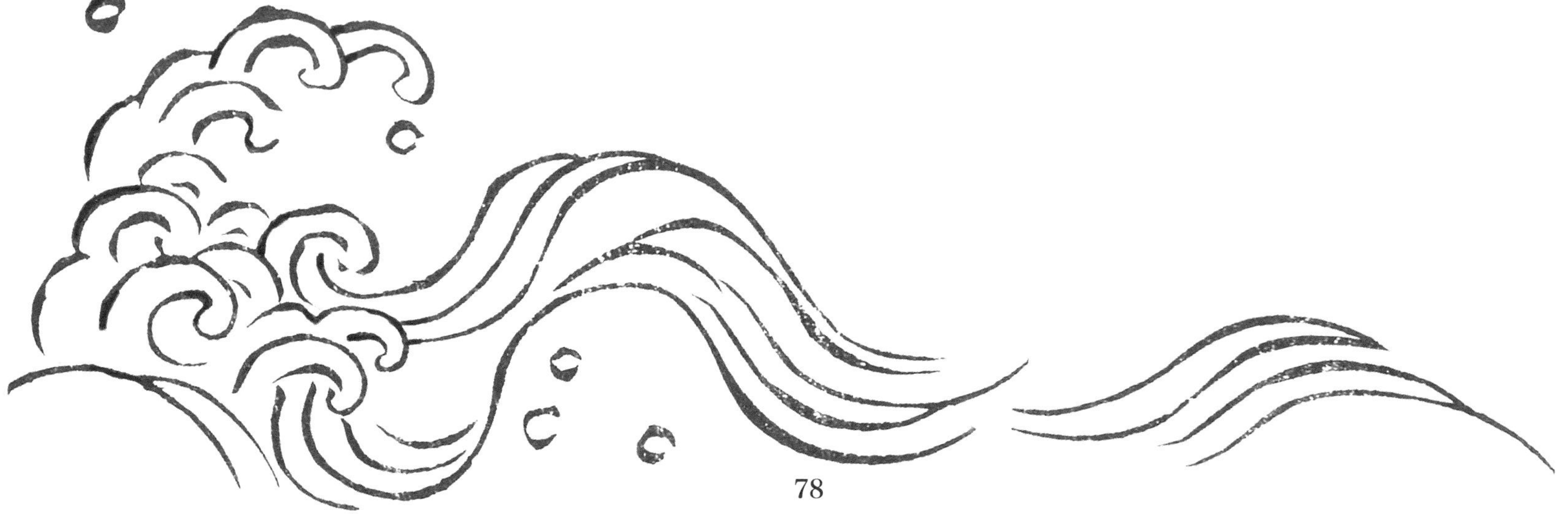

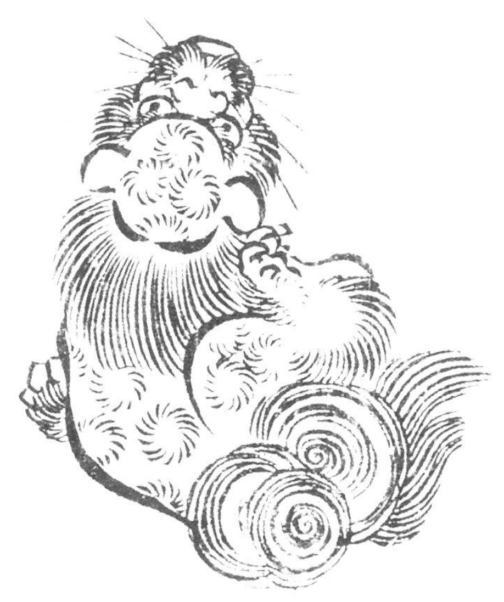

Art by Katsushika Hokusai

Edited by Jocelyn Norbury and Gary Panton
Designed by Zoe Bradley
Cover designed by Angie Allison
With special thanks to Professor Timon Screech

Manufacturer: First published in Great Britain in 2026 by LOM ART, an imprint of
Michael O'Mara Books Limited, 9 Lion Yard, Tremadoc Road, London SW4 7NQ
www.mombooks.com

Represented by: Authorised Rep Compliance Ltd, Ground Floor,
71 Lower Baggot Street, Dublin D02 P593, Ireland
www.arccompliance.com

 www.mombooks.com/lom 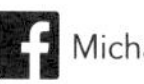 Michael O'Mara Books 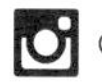 @lomart.books

A CIP catalogue record for this book is available from the British Library.

ISBN: 978-1-915751-49-2

1 3 5 7 9 10 8 6 4 2

This product is made of material from well-managed, FSC®-certified
forests and other controlled sources. The manufacturing processes
conform to the environmental regulations of the country of origin.

Printed in Dubai, UAE.

For further information see www.mombooks.com/about/sustainability-climate-focus
Report any safety issues to product.safety@mombooks.com